IF MONEY
COULD TALK

IF MONEY COULD TALK

Pecuniae Cause

M. L. Marcos

IF MONEY COULD TALK

Copyright © 2019 M. L. Marcos.

All rights reserved. No part of this book may be used or reproduced by any means, graphic, electronic, or mechanical, including photocopying, recording, taping or by any information storage retrieval system without the written permission of the author except in the case of brief quotations embodied in critical articles and reviews.

iUniverse books may be ordered through booksellers or by contacting:

iUniverse
1663 Liberty Drive
Bloomington, IN 47403
www.iuniverse.com
1-800-Authors (1-800-288-4677)

Because of the dynamic nature of the Internet, any web addresses or links contained in this book may have changed since publication and may no longer be valid. The views expressed in this work are solely those of the author and do not necessarily reflect the views of the publisher, and the publisher hereby disclaims any responsibility for them.

Any people depicted in stock imagery provided by Getty Images are models, and such images are being used for illustrative purposes only.
Certain stock imagery © Getty Images.

ISBN: 978-1-5320-6716-7 (sc)
ISBN: 978-1-5320-6717-4 (hc)
ISBN: 978-1-5320-6718-1 (e)

Library of Congress Control Number: 2019900933

Print information available on the last page.

iUniverse rev. date: 05/18/2019

To Jasmin, Frederic, Liza, and Nomi, and to the memory of Norma

CONTENTS

Acknowledgments xiii
Introduction xv

Chapter 1   Money Concepts 1
   Income Source 1: Employment 17
   Income Source 2: Business 26
   Income Source 3: Self-Employment 30
  The Monetary Influences 32
   Parents 33
   The School System 36
   Government 39
   Our Own Research 40
   From Other People 41
   From Books/Internet 41
  The Side Effects of Welfare 42
  The Bottom Line 43

Chapter 2   Business Theories 47
  Why? 49
   Business Advantages 57
   Business Disadvantages 59
  Who? 61
   Ability to Make Decisions 63
   Responsibility 66

    Economic Level 68
    Capabilities of the Risk-Takers 71
    Chutzpah: Only Qualification You Will Ever Need 73
    Leadership 74
    Ability to Communicate 75
When? 77
    The Age Factor 78
    The Health Factor 79
    The Race Factor 80
How to Start a Business 82
    The First Step 82
    The Invention Theory 84
    The Importation Theory 85
    The Service Business Theory 87
    The College Project Theory 87
    The Knowledge Factor Theory 88
How to Manage a Business 89
    No Experience Required 90
    The Professional Help 91
    The Lawyer 92
    The Accountant 93
    The Banker 94
How to Maintain 96
    Recruit, Train, and Retain 96
    To Delegate or Not to Delegate 98

Chapter 3   Business Development 102
    The Conception 106
    The Gestation Period 108
    The Birth 109
    The Growing Pains 109
    Maturity 110

Sale or Demise 111
    A Case in Point 112
The Brain 116
The Plan 118
The Idea 120
The Evolution of a Business 123
    The Computer Bits and Bytes 124
    The Automobile Track 126
    Food for Thought 127
    The Subdivision and Specialty 129
    The Storefront 130
    The Internet or Mail Order 131
    The Multilevel and Pyramid Schemes 131
Something to Think About 136

Chapter 4   Financing a Business 137
The Chicken-and-Egg Syndrome 138
The Financing Cycle 144
    The Five *C*s of Financing 144
        Credit Rating 145
        Capital 147
        Collateral 149
        Capabilities 150
        Vicious Circle of Credit 151
        Character 152
Credit: The Lifeblood of Our Economy 153
    The Right Bank 153
    The Credit Application 154
    The Projections 155
    The Financial Statements 156
        The Balance Sheet 156
    Venture Capitalist 157
    Wealthy Friends and Relatives 157

Chapter 5   Sales and Marketing 158
   Marketing.. 162
      It Pays to Be First.. 163
      What Is in a Name?... 164
      Specialize... 165
      Perception.. 166
   Sales... 166
      Are Salespeople Made or Born?....................................... 167
      The Appointment 168
         Create the Need 169
         Make the Customer Want It...................................... 171
         Going for the Close 172
   Lessons According to the Experts....................................... 174
      Do Not Argue 175
      Words to Avoid.. 175
      Service, Service, Service... 176
      Marketing, Sales, and Money 177

Chapter 6   Motivation 178
   The Conscious and Subconscious Minds 179
   Desire 181
   Knowledge... 183
   Action 188
   The Unfortunate Environment 190

Chapter 7   Checklists 193
   Business Credit Application 195
   Sample Projection 196
   Financial Statements 196
   Money Advice..200

Chapter 8   Conclusion 201
   Belief 210
   Commitment... 212

    Dedication, Desire, and Decision..212
    Energy 213
    Faith 213
    Goal Setting.. 213
    Your Own Inspiration Words... 215
    Finally, Back to Basics... 216

Appendix 219
Book Review 221
About the Author..225

ACKNOWLEDGMENTS

Appreciation is expressed to a dear friend, Rome Ibera, for his encouragement and invaluable assistance in completing this book.

INTRODUCTION

The most coveted commodity is undoubtedly the legal tender popularly known as the banknote created by the Federal Reserve or the central bank of most countries. It is versatile, convertible, and valuable by design. Life as we know it would not be conducive without the convenience and benefit it brings.

The internet of today has a new entrant called cryptocurrency, or Bitcoin, whose mechanism can be understood only by the selected few and is not backed by any government. However, it is gaining acceptance, especially among those involved in the internet trade who are well versed in its algorithm; therefore it is not covered in this book. One can get Bitcoins by purchasing them with their hard-earned dollars with the added advantage that the cryptocurrency is publicly traded; therefore, the intrinsic value may increase or decrease.

Money as a medium of exchange is as ubiquitous as a house key in that its absence can cause deep depression and unhappiness. It is so important that one must not or cannot leave home without it, as per advice of American Express like its card system. It is the most important accessory of any Gucci or Louis Vuitton purse and an indispensable lining to one's wallet.

It is so important that its value, like one's blood pressure, should not read too low because arrhythmia will be triggered if left below the acceptable standard. This sad case of penuriousness—though not necessarily fatal—will gnaw on one's physical and mental health.

There is a humorous story of a tycoon who got hit with the generous bug and decided to lessen his financial burden by giving a quarter from his fortune to charity.

Now the amount of his wealth is twenty-five cents less! Facetious maybe, but Rockefeller, one of the original billionaires, distributed dimes in his spare time.

To know the multitude of legal ways of supplementing your cash pile is not very difficult if you are familiar with the equivalency of money, which is the exact mission statement of this book.

The catchphrase of 2018 by the democratic left is that "socialism works." This belief by the young generation is a flagrant misunderstanding of the principle of what money is all about. The millennials erred in their egregious belief that education, jobs, health care, food, and the like can be provided free of charge by the government as an inalienable right for everyone to enjoy. The rationale is that these responsibilities are to be paid by government taxes and the wealthy people. But who pays the taxes? This entitlement mantra has been spreading its tentacles like seaweed in the open seas. But as is the case with the Great Barrier Reef, there are sharks lurking in the nooks and crannies of the ocean floor.

Countries such as Kuwait could afford to spoil their citizens with outlandish perks because Allah made sure that their real estate is sitting on an invaluable liquid gold. Besides, they deny all migrants the right to become permanent residents, let alone citizens, by imposing stringent qualifications for naturalization and selective parentage birthright. Their population growth is also negligible.

Pundits say that countries with socialist programs are doing quite well. Unknown to them, the residents are levied with hefty taxes, which hardworking inhabitants would not welcome or pay for. "My neighbors should pay the bill." Unbeknownst to them, the neighbors were saying the same thing. Sooner or later, the piper must be paid. Former president Reagan said that socialism only works in two places—in heaven, where they do not need it, and in hell, where they already have it.

In the second half of 2008, the worst recession since the Great Depression of October 1929 to 1933, began to roar like a raging bull. The result of this global problem is that people's savings and wealth have disappeared overnight. Financial newspapers talked about billions of dollars lost in the stock markets. How did it happen, and where did the money go?

While many of us cling to the belief that money is the root of all evil, no one can deny that greed, especially excessive avarice without just compensation, has caused the evaporation of wealth. Unfortunately, the evildoers were not necessarily the victims but at times were richly rewarded for being the catalyst of these disastrous maneuvers. These financial gurus make money whether the trend is up or down.

Therefore, if money could talk, just exactly what would it tell us about what went wrong?

The hope is if we learn the reasons for these lost fortunes, then we can avoid or minimize their devastating effects. We do not want history to repeat itself.

We all want to live in comfort, free of financial worries, and to be able to buy most, if not all, of the things we want and need! This suggests that our income must exceed our expenses or at the very least equal our expenditures.

Yet only a selected few are granted this wish. They are the elite group of individuals who are providentially favored to be the recipients of a healthy ratio of income over expenses. Is it possible to be included in this august body so that we can achieve our personal economic nirvana?

I believe so—if we learn and implement the laws that govern the process of how to accomplish our pecuniary goals. We could then set a bull's-eye target of achievement of at least $1 million in assets.

Unbeknownst to the majority of the population, the earth's wealth and resources have been equitably divided among all the people, not according to their needs or wants but according to their direct participation or nonparticipation in the pursuit of wealth acquisition. This is a case of every man for himself. It is extremely easy to spot who those fortunate people are just by looking around for outstanding individuals in their jobs or businesses, family standards, and social statuses in the community.

Maybe this is to ensure a healthy world order, or it's the lack of willingness among people to alter the socially imposed proportion. It has remained numerically steady and is not likely to be changed for the foreseeable future. Before we discuss the course of action to take to improve our lives, let us see where we belong in the food chain hierarchy.

This book is intended as an eye-opener to the exciting world of wealth accumulation. Since everyone has their level of financial satisfaction, the amount therefore is not of prime concern. Only you can decide your fortune in direct proportion to your unique dreams.

Readers are advised to expand their knowledge by reading other books dedicated solely to specific areas of interest, such as business planning, accounting, personal desires, and so forth.

The Troika of Civilization

Society, since the beginning of time, has categorized the troika of the civilization based on a socioeconomic hierarchy in the shape of a pyramid. This geometric figure may have an illegal connotation, but all organizations and companies adhere to this configuration. Maybe that is why even the necropolis structures of Egypt are shaped like a cone, to tell us that the same is true in the great beyond.

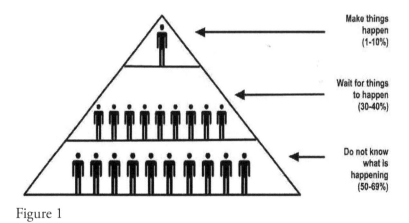

Figure 1

They Make Things Happen

In the building blocks of society, the doers are designed to be the spires and foundation (about 5 percent approximately). Though this number is variable in different countries, in North America, the popular guess is about 1 percent. They are laid out architecturally to be the solid base and be the zenith, in control and in charge. These are the only places they could fit in—as if to declare to the whole world that without their directions, the structures underneath or above them will fall into disarray.

While there is always room at the top, only a handful of people belong there simply because only the brave have the courage, innovative ability, and appropriate know-how to get there. They are the ones who have discovered and mastered the use of the Archimedean lever long enough to move the world.

They are the pillars of the economy. They are the inventors of all things that are useful to improve our lives such as light bulbs, computers, machineries, automobiles, appliances, and so on.

They are referred to as the prime movers of the universe!

These people do not just perch in the wayside reluctantly doing nothing. When given the chance to choreograph a dance routine in tune to the beat of any music, they solicit the divine help of St. Vitus to create a pattern of rhythmic steps. They do not sit down to vegetate, but they spring into action. This energetic group will do their best to improvise graceful moves in time with the beat. They are active, dynamic, and proactive, always finding possibilities. Instead of asking the obvious question "Why?", they ask the productive inquiry, "Why not?"

In this mobile and competitive world, they are the drivers of Formula One and Indy cars who have set their sights on the checkered flag. They are aware that only one contestant will drive the victory lap. If luck is not on their side this time, that doesn't discourage them from contending again, for win or lose, they will be back to compete another day. Winning is not a onetime deal. Losing is just a temporary setback.

While the grand prize may elude them more often than not, they take solace in the thought that they did all the necessary physical and mental preparations to raise their odds for the opportunity to stand in the winner's circle, preferably sooner rather than later.

There is no such thing as a perfunctory race. They are meticulous in planning. They spare no expense for victory and practice as often as they can. They love the dangers, thrive on competing, and believe that these are only obstacles and not failures. To the winners, *success* is not just a onetime thing; it is every day and everything.

Andrew Carnegie of the steel industry, J. P. Morgan of banking, Henry Ford of automobiles, Thomas Watson of the computer, Sam Walton of retail, and Thomas Edison of household appliances are a few entrepreneurs of the industrial revolution generation who made things happen.

Bill Gates, Sergey Brin, Michael Dell, and Elon Musk are some of the living individuals included in the list of people who have made the most of the same Archimedean lever; that is why their names are indelibly etched in the financial history books as business world innovators. They are members of the elite group who have innovated our lives. They created labor-saving things that altered our modus vivendi.

With their contributions, life has tremendously improved and been enhanced—no longer a boring routine. We were introduced to new business activities, electronic equipments, and machineries. We are now more efficient, productive, and mobile.

In communities around the country and the world, people are quietly making things happen. They do not make waves or have banners but are working inconspicuously hard. They keenly observe and experiment with the multitude of ways to create products or services for others to use and enjoy.

An inconspicuous garage in your neighborhood like 367 Addison Avenue, Palo Alto, California, address of Hewlett Packard could become as famous as 2066 Crist Drive, Los Altos, California. If the latter address does not ring a bell to you, this is where the trillion-dollar company Apple (based on August 18, 2018, Yahoo News, with market capitalization of $1.05 trillion) had its beginnings. Like the house of Rembrandt in Amsterdam where he painted most of his masterpieces, the 2066 Crist Drive residence is now a museum.

They discovered that being productive in society is financially rewarding, not to mention the self-fulfillment they enjoy at the end of the day. They are the firm believers of gracious living and eventually leave this world a better place for their fellow human beings and for the next generation. (Google search their biographies, and you will read their accomplishments.)

They learn at an early age that whatever they do must benefit others, otherwise people will not compensate them accordingly. J. Paul Getty discovered oil deposits, pumped out the black liquid gold, and then refined it to gas up the cars of others. He attributed his success by telling people that some will find gushers while others find dry wells.

Was Getty just plain lucky to be endowed with the discriminating nose to sniff the aroma of oil like the chemist of Galimard perfumery? Or did he develop the uncanny ability to drill in the right location of mineral deposits? Getty's father, Franklin, was a successful oilman himself who relocated his family close to where the drilling activities were in Oklahoma and California. J. Paul Getty was not only in the right place; under the guidance of his father, he successfully honed his uncanny ability to pinpoint where potential "gushers" were.

Getty and others like him worked hard to produce products and services that benefited others. The beneficiaries and users of these products and services are members of the second category.

Waiting for Things to Happen

(See figure 1)

The guesstimate of this bunch is about 45 percentile. The second group refers to the group of desultorious individuals who start out on life's journey not knowing where to go and end up life not knowing where they have been.

As in any social group, there are passive or easygoing individuals who would rather see others do the unpleasant work and heavy lifting. They stay on the sidelines like frightened turtles with their heads and extremities safely tucked in the safety of their shells. Restrained and secured, they could not move a muscle even if they want to. Is it because they are afraid to fail or to do something they will regret?

Fear is the monster in you that feeds on confusion; it is a paralyzing four-letter word that festers ambitious minds. Like our amphibian example, they see the activities around them through a peephole, silently and inconspicuously. At the very least, our amphibious amigo does it for a good reason—to stifle the prey.

They do not realize that finding the financial talisman sometimes requires them to perform uncomfortable and unpleasant acts like kissing a toad, as in Disney's Prince Charming. The act alone, compared to the many things we have to do in life, is a very unpleasant and warty experience, but if that is the solution to our earthly miseries, then we should ignore the temporary incommode, especially if that is the only way we can work our magic charms. To change means doing something you are not used to.

They have learned that success is sweetest to those who struggle to win, for there is no royal road to success. It could be long and winding, with sharp pebbles and potholes before you hit the mother lode. It does not belong to the faint of heart or to those who seem content in any situation. These weak-kneed people need others to stimulate them into action; otherwise, they are lackadaisical, contented, indolent people, nurturing their placid personalities.

They are the wallflowers of the dance floor, only to regret later that they did not participate in the party merrymaking. They are the party poopers. They claim to be sports minded, but they just love to be spectators. They would not swing a racquet or throw a ball, for they are terminally ill with a devastating permanent condition called incurable tennis elbow.

They are the gullible recipients of letters from a deposed Nigerian king telling them that a pot of gold awaits them at the end of the African rainbow. All they need to do is disclose their bank account information so that they can receive their much-coveted bonanza via electronic transfer.

They are big fans of the lotto management who promise them that they will never stop selling the magic numbers until everybody becomes a millionaire, and most especially them, the gullible ones. They never pass by a lottery kiosk where lady luck did not smile or call their attention. They sincerely believe that one day the winning numbers will be revealed in their dreams, which will allow them to join the ranks of the upper 10 percent—the movers.

Making choices is one of the fundamental rights God has given us. We have many options to take in this life. Unfortunately, this group would rather watch others do the innovative work. They may feel incapable, unskilled, or not intelligent enough to do or produce anything of value.

They are the cheerleaders, always ready to applaud, carry the modernizer on their shoulders, and organize the fan club to place the victor on a pedestal.

Since childhood, we have heard it a thousand times: we must learn how to wait, and our turn will come. Infinite patience is a saintly virtue. Good things come to those who wait. These are all well-intentioned pieces of advice that are overlooked by the outstanding achievers.

The issue is, What and Who are we waiting for? Positive events in our lives were not scheduled like the airline reservation system so that all activities are properly interconnected. Our lives were not laid out by a computer programmer who drew a biological flowchart that will only produce a positive result. If that was the case, we would all be living prosperous and productive lives.

Like a good sniper, we wait for the appropriate target, but for how long? Sooner or later, we get bored and tired. What is frustrating and difficult to accept is the fact that we do not know the activities happening on the other side of the spectrum. They may have all the fun!

Unaware of What's Happening

(See figure 1)

Proportioned at approximately 50 percent, this group at the bottom end makes up the rest of the troika. Combining the two levels underneath the apex of the social pyramid are the overwhelming majority.

"The majority rules" is a democratic truism that stood the test of time. If the number of those who agree is above the median, then they must be doing or saying the right things. Is this true especially in the process of financial management?

While ignorance is bliss, these people may find out too late that they should have done or known more, especially in the field of wealth acquisition. They comprise the base and bigger part of the economic pyramid—those that are easily influenced by popular people such as movie stars, talk show hosts, and church leaders. For this reason, the politicians strive to focus their benevolence to them primarily because they could make or break a political career by their sheer numbers.

The motivations of these politicians may be selfish, but this accentuates the fact that there are more people with eyes focused on survival and short-term interests than those who have visions of a prosperous future.

This social segment's transformation to becoming productive members of society is the focus of this book. This manuscript aims to help in the basic understanding of successful money-earning activities. At the very least, the intention is to help readers learn how to afford the basic necessities of life and, if successful, to pay for the luxurious items we desire.

We accomplish this by understanding who we are on the rung of the social pyramid, the limits imposed by our society at large at the different economic strata, and how to overcome them. We must educate ourselves. We must spare no expense for that goal. If you get discouraged, remember that remaining naive will leave you as dry as the tundra of the arctic or as desolate as the desert of Patagonia.

Education is the solution to most problems, whether they are social or economic. Knowledge is power! It is the most powerful tool we can use in life.

It is interesting to note that the most knowledgeable people have an edge over those who hang into ignorance.

To be prepared is to have an idea of what to do and to be able to accurately predict what would happen when given the right parameters. These people don't do haphazard work. If they do, they make an educated guess.

It is little surprise, then, that one business catchphrase runs like this: "The educated consumer is our best customer." People who know what they want do not waste time going over an infinite number of choices. That would be like trying to find a needle in a haystack. Smart consumers, being educated, simply segregate the hay and find the needle right away because they know what they want and where to find it in the first place.

They don't rely merely on chance or luck. Therefore, they minimize surprises because they know what to expect. If there are fewer surprises, there are better chances for success. A knowledgeable person can make more effective plans for contingencies in case they occur. Minimizing uncertainties is the secret of successful wealth acquisition.

We fear ambiguity, just as most of us fear death, because we know nothing of the great beyond. What is in store for us? We do not know; that's why we're scared. But if you know what is there, and you know what to expect, then fear is considerably attenuated. We become more courageous because we are no longer working in the dark areas, minimizing obscurity.

If we are afraid, we get paralyzed from the tip of our hair to our toes. We can't move; we stagnate and in the process develop bedsores from the vicious cycle of mendicancy—that is, blaming others instead of ourselves. We do not realize that when we point that index finger at others, we are pointing the other three fingers at ourselves, the real culprits.

Poignant Reality

To borrow the parlance of the sports world, the misunderstanding of the equivalence of money is the unforced error of the essence of life. Money is not the ground zero of evil but ignorance of its facsimile.

The lesson of the above in tennis, for example, is the difficulty for a neophyte to return a simple serve, no matter how hard he or she tries. The trajectories are haphazard, the strength employed could be weak or overpowering, and the player is off-balance or off-target.

Let us look at some of the alternative solutions when we want to raise some funds—a euphemism for borrowing.

The economy of the world today revolves on the ease of credit to fund our purchases. The gross domestic product of any country depends on the availability of funds on credit.

During my university days, my parents had many financial concerns, especially since there were seven of us attending school at the same time. Oftentimes our tuition fees exceeded their savings and income. The solution employed during those budgeting crises required the uncanny ability of my mother to find and borrow money from a person willing to help with our fiscal dilemma. In the Philippines, the other handy remedy is to write and solicit free help from an overseas relative to pay the shortfalls.

The same is true when we want to purchase goods or services, and funds are not available. We have to look for people or businesses willing to grant us credit.

The problem is that like all credit, it becomes payable. For some, there are no problems because they could easily pay the full amount or the required installments. What do we do, then, if we cannot? Sadly for some of us, we fall into the debt traps wherein the bankruptcy arbitrators are not far behind, ringing our alarm bell.

The ratio of wealthy over poor is so low that in the third world or the developing world this is common. Is this the time for humankind to act and do something about this financial imbalance?

Who is to be blamed? Society? To whom can we point the finger? Should there be a fall guy? Would that change anything? More importantly, would it solve the dilemma?

The communists used to blame the capitalists. Communism tends to equalize everybody's standards by depressing the common person's ability to shine economically unless one is a high-ranking member of the politburo. Now communism has converted and metamorphosed into democratic society. A fresh set of 10 percent movers and shakers has been created.

The new 90 percent are now confused and do not know what to do. Some are longing for the good old days, while others are crying all the phobias known to men.

The verity of it is that these movers and shakers are not necessarily by providential right that automatically entrusted their membership in the new society. It is true that some may not deserve to be included in the affluent group.

Being at the right place at the right time is a common impression. Could we influence lady luck to recommend us to be included in this privileged organization?

Making or Earning a Living

First, we have to understand and learn the rules for membership in this elite group. The requirement is to own plenty of "dough"—euphemism for money.

We need money, sometimes plenty, to affect the changes we want to implement. It is just like going to war; we need ammunition to convince our nemesis of our point of view; we need remunerations for our soldiers and for allies to agree to join forces with us.

We may not have the funds, especially at the beginning, or enough of it to do the things we want. Therefore, we need to first learn the techniques of earning and the art of accumulating financial armament, better known as wealth.

The art of accumulating money is difficult at best. It means a complete transformation in our beliefs, attitudes, and character. We have to learn difficult, unfamiliar, and uncomfortable skills. These unique skills, rules, and knowledge are essential in the world of money and finance.

The monetary realm has its own bylaws and language. If you have to learn another tongue, you might as well master the lingo of currency.

It oftentimes comes in handy, like the story of the cornered mouse with an ability to mimic a dog, allowing him and his bunch of mice to escape. The moral is that it pays to speak another lingua franca.

You never know when your opportunity knocks. However, there are many ways and techniques, both legal and illegal.

This book is about knowing the important principles, as set forth by society at large, the community you live in, and the government. Familiarity with and the adoption of these principles will help you raise your standard of living, position you in a comfortable place in society, and give you the ability to live an enjoyable and meaningful life.

Biologically, you need air and water to maintain your life. These are two of the basic necessities to survive. You do not need to understand the origin and composition of water and air. Nature has provided air free of charge, and you pay only for water deliveries. Consequently, you take them for granted, especially since you cannot see or taste the air around you, and you can conveniently turn a tap to acquire a seemingly endless amount of water.

Our forefathers devised the monetary system to facilitate the movement of goods and the rendering of services. The monetary system is a method of accounting for the value of all the goods and services we have provided to others.

The amount of money we have is a direct representation of the total values of those goods and services rendered to others.

It is, therefore, reasonable to state that people with plenty of money must have given plenty of equivalent goods and rendered corresponding services. These people who are affluent, wealthy, prosperous, and rich are prolific providers of useful things.

Well-to-do people fascinate us. We envy them. We adore them. Yet, at the same time, we despise them. The difference in the standard of living between the rich and the poor is wider than ever. The rich are getting richer. The poor are getting poorer! That is the general feeling. Is that belief justified? Never in the history of civilization has so much wealth been owned by so few, paraphrasing Churchill.

But why is there a big disparity? How could the majority be willing to share the crumbs while the wealthy minorities are living a life of excessive abundance? It is obvious that the 5 percent know something the majority is not aware of. Are the affluent elite deliberately keeping the secrets of wealth? Could it be that the majority refuses to find out the reasons for the huge difference in the economic standards of living? Is it too difficult to learn and understand?

The meaning of the phrase "financial freedom" differs among individuals. Members of the same family will not have the same interpretations, let alone people of different races, creeds, genders, and personalities. Individual differences play a very crucial role in determining the financial level one requires to live a comfortable life. Regardless of the amount one needs to have a satisfactory life and to maintain a lifestyle, we all want to have the ability to buy the goods and services we like for ourselves and our families to maintain a comfortable living.

The idea of financial freedom is not new. The manner of achieving it is probably elementary to some people. Yet the question is why are there so many poor people living below the poverty line? Why do so many people have difficulty paying their bills and declare bankruptcy? Why are there so many employees who are unhappy with their income and getting sick of worry?

The answer to this is that people do not know how to earn enough money for their personal needs. Most people do not understand the mechanics of what money is, where it comes from, and, most importantly, how to get their fair share. Happiness is earning more money than you can spend or, at the very least, balancing the money you earn with the money you spend.

Money is a five-letter word that can be found in everybody's language and pocketbooks. It is the same nonapothecary remedy needed to revive Thurston Howell III on *Gilligan's Island* when he fainted or Mr. Drysdale of *Beverly Hillbillies* fame. There is no doubt that all the people of the world have touched and used money. Every palm, living or dead, has been greased by money (legally, that is). But what does money really represent, and, more importantly, how can you earn it?

Our forefathers shaped the government, formed the Constitution, and, most importantly, established the economy. In the United States of America, Thomas Jefferson and company set the framework of the US economy and created US legal tender bills and the dollar coins.

Willingly or inadvertently, the US dollar coin gave us the clue to financial freedom and prosperity. What is the rationale for the symbol and the meaning of the Latin phrase used, "E pluribus unum"?

This book, like the US dollar coin, has adopted the eagle as part of our logo. The eagle signifies pride, aggressiveness, and self-confidence. "Fly and be cunning like an eagle, and avoid the flight formation of turkeys" is sage advice. You have to possess those traits to acquire money.

Under the symbol is the Latin phrase "e pluribus unum." What in the world does that mean? Why use a dead language that few people understand? Is this a cryptic message for the privileged few, who are entitled to receive the almighty dollar and who are entitled to have the majority of the nation's wealth? The national bird gave us the succinct answer "out of many, one"—e pluribus unum!

On this book cover, we used this phrase as our mantra: "pecuniae cause" (for the sake of wealth). The process of accumulating money is to understand the rules of wealth building. If we know the necessary steps to raising our economic standards, we can enjoy the journey to financial independence.

A race car driver must be thoroughly familiar with his or her racing machine. He or she has to know all the car's idiosyncrasies so he or she can tell when everything is running smoothly and can correct accurately whatever goes wrong. The same is true with wealth building.

Familiarizing yourself with the concepts of money is what musicians call a five-finger exercise. Having gone this far, it is safe to assume that you have the passion of a convert to become wealth conscious, willing to avail yourself of life's potential gold mine. This book offers you a gilded invitation to read the whole agenda in the following pages.

If money could talk, it would tell us to financially rock our prosperity consciousness and roll our dollar bills in bundles.

CHAPTER 1

Money Concepts

Let's start from the very beginning, as recommended by Rodgers and Hammerstein in one of their lyrics in *The Sound of Music*. When you commence your literacy quest, you first learn the alphabet. When you want to learn how to sing, you first have to learn the musical scale.

To become a champion pugilist, one has to learn the theory and science of punch throwing and avoidance. He must learn to absorb right or left hook punches that did not miss. Likewise, money concepts must be learned before wealth accumulation can happen. To the people who purport to be knowledgeable about money matters, this topic might be elementary, simple and sophomoric. Think of this as Economics 101.

If money could only talk, it would tell us exactly what we need to do in order to amass any amount we desire. The prized rectangular-shaped legal tender would tell us the step-by-step procedure by which we can partake in this bounty. How do we proceed? What is the first step?

Before the first seven-star hotel, Burj Al Arab was erected in Dubai; its chief architect, Tom Wright of WS Atkins PLC, must have pondered with intense interest and focused like the Hubble telescope lens. Mr. Wright with his army of first-rate architects would have laid out the precise structural design instructions and list of top-notch materials in order to translate his innovative blueprint on the drawing board into stark reality. This would have been an invaluable help for the general contractors and civil engineers. Otherwise, the construction would have been shoddy or a downright fiasco in the extremely demanding eyes of the owner, the sultan of UAE, the discriminating critics, and the viewing public.

The preparations expended were formidable, but the result was like the legendary phoenix rising out of its ashes, ascending from the sand dunes of Jumeirah Beach. Nowhere would you find a more admirable landmark and feast for the eyes than this construction, a masterpiece of a genius—the Burj Khalifa, icon of Dubai. Presidents, state dignitaries, and other renowned people in the know are simply amazed and are in awe as the princely accommodations take their breath away. This hotel accepts Arab Emirates dinars (AEDs), the denomination of choice for this one-of-a-kind seven-star hotel. It is so exclusive that management charges admission just to enter the premises; at least they offer free drinks for the privilege.

With a sandy foundation, one would think that construction of anything so gargantuan in that area would be a virtual impossibility. Rising sixty floors with an exoskeleton composed of Teflon-coated fiberglass cloth is an allusion to the biblical admonition not to build one's house on sand but on solid rock for it to last. Indeed, it would be tantamount to building a castle in the air with plumbing made of pipe dreams. Instead, we have a historic jewel of a landmark in the Arabian Sea. It takes several hours of television shows to detail the preparations needed to cover all the historic edifices of Dubai.

"Preparation and foresight is the key," the students of the CIA and FBI would say in emphatic unison, for they have been brainwashed to accept it as a mantra in their chosen cooking careers. These students from the Culinary Institute of America (CIA) and the Food & Beverage Institute (FBI) of South Africa know that a food that is worth salivating over or to sink your teeth into should be prepared with the necessary choice ingredients available and presented with unreserved attractive presentation. A feast to the eyes is a delight to the palate.

The same students are instructed from day one about the culinary art of understanding the nutritional value of the different food ingredients. Likewise, the effects of the gamut of condiments and spices can change the palette of menu colors into varying combinations to produce an irresistible culinary *obra maestra*. This sounds like advice of the late Anthony Bourdain, TV host of *No Reservations* and *Parts Unknown*, but it is true!

They follow a definite pattern of recipes as instructed by their expert mentors until they themselves could formulate or modify their own as they are taught to think critically and independently. These are all guaranteed to satisfy the discriminating taste of a gastronome.

It should come as no surprise if such preparation and foresight are more paramount in the federal agencies bearing the same acronyms. The obvious reason is that lives and not taste buds are on the line. The end result shows a significant reduction in margin of error and fatality.

Experts of the game of pool are able to predict the trajectory of the cue ball and its final position to be able to pocket the next shot. To know the geometrical pattern of the white ball's travel and the actions that the cue ball will take separates the amateur from the specialist. In life, we should prepare like the whiz of pool. Paul Newman (Fast Eddie) and Jackie Gleason (Fats Domino) made this very clear in the movie *The Hustler*.

Chess competitions demonstrate the crucial need for preparation. Grandmasters plan every possible move and combination in advance, sometimes by the dozen. Each step is designed to accomplish the goal to checkmate the king and to anticipate the countermoves their opponents are going to take based on set algorithms and countermoves.

Every push of a piece on the chessboard is a preparation for their plans and counteracts the opponent's anticipated retaliation. Be it an attempt to annihilate the castle, kidnap the queen, euthanize the royal horse, disgrace the bishop, or amputate the soldiers, it has a single goal: to vanquish the king. For this, they have to make intelligent guesses about what the other players will do in the next couple of moves, all under time limit and pressure.

The more they can accurately foresee opponent strategy, the better their chances of winning. Again, nothing is happenstance. Everything is a result of planned preparation, hard work, and focused determination.

The popular TV show *Iron Chef* illustrates the lesson succinctly. "Iron" is, of course, an appropriate description of either their utensils or their determination to win or both. The competing chefs must come up with their best menus from a surprise list of ingredients, or so the program producers want their viewers to believe.

These iron chefs must browse through their mental cooking encyclopedias to create unsurpassed gourmet meals that will titillate the palates of the discerning panel of judges. Necessarily, the menus have to be above par, taste and presentation wise. The winning entry would be determined by the number of senses that the concoction will most satisfy.

The same is true with life. It is not a spectator sport. It is a competition that needs preparation and proactive participation, not passivity. In the words of Socrates, the sage Greek philosopher of yore, an unexamined life is not worth living.

It has been said that we only live twice, once when we are born and the other when we are staring death in the face. Realistically though, we have only one chance to live a successful life. What we do with our individual lives is our own business. But there's the rub; this involves the painful words "our responsibility."

No matter how long we live, life is short compared to eternity or to the age of the galaxy.

Should that make us despair and say, What's the use of trying so hard if everything we do is so insignificant?" Only the coward or the faint of heart will say that. Whenever they find themselves in the boiler room of competition, it is a major disturbance of their comfort zones. They are scared of any type of contest because they feel they are losers. They were born with low expectations and self-esteem. They are pessimistic, thinking that the other guy always wins and always dates the prom queen. They stay out of the kitchen because they cannot stand the heat.

Yet, whether we realize it or not, we are in constant competition. The Olympics of life is not only to contend with others but against ourselves of yesteryears.

The catchphrase of a US presidential candidate simply asked, "Are you better off today?" Even if you voted for him, it is possible that your economic situation may not have improved by simply relying on the battle cry of the election.

Unless we understand the building blocks of prosperity, it is difficult to alter our financial destinies. We have to be educated with the brick and mortar of affluence, which is *money*.

Supposedly, everyone knows what money is. We use it daily. Most of our time is spent chasing what the majority of us refer to as the almighty buck, dough, quid, or whatever your culture prefers to use as its idiom. As soon as a child can form complete sentences, probably the first one is, "I want milk." "Please give me money" is probably not far behind.

The main function of this book is to make clear to the reader what money is all about. We realize that everyone, except hermits, has used money.

This book is intended to make readers understand what money equates to. More importantly, what does money really stand for or represent?

Water is a life-giving and life-saving liquid. The animals of Africa risk their lives visiting waterholes. Many of us drink water every day, save those who prefer wine and beer, but even these fermentations are composed mainly of water.

We take water for granted because it is readily available. All we need to do is to turn our faucets and the thirst-quenching liquid flows freely. But what should we do if the plumbing or the stream runs dry? We may be forced to chemically produce water.

Water is two parts hydrogen and one part oxygen, hence H_2O. As long as you have these two components in the right proportions, you will always come up with water.

The most important question is do you know how to produce or where to get the raw components to make water? Two atoms of hydrogen and one atom of oxygen?

If we know the chemical process of combining hydrogen and oxygen, we can manufacture an unlimited amount of water for our use and sell the excess production for income and profit.

Unfortunately, the production of money is not a simple process of just printing your own. The US Mint is the only one allowed by law to print the US dollar. If you do, your dream residence will be a house with eight-by-six-foot rooms with curtains made of iron bars.

The reality is we cannot make money legally! We can only earn it, inherit it, or have it given to us willingly. This means that one has to understand the mechanics of wealth accumulation, a system that has eluded the majority of the population.

The denotation of money is coin, silver, gold, or other metal stamped by public authority and used as a medium of exchange. In a wider sense, it is any equivalent for commodities for which individuals readily exchange their goods and services. King Croesus of the ancient country of Lydia allegedly minted the first silver and gold coin from 560 to 540 BC.

It is important to note that money or any of its equivalents such as precious metal and objects are accepted in lieu of the actual goods and services. Even today, in some part of Africa, salt is still used. The word "salary" is derived from the Latin word *sal*.

Similarly, "pecuniary" comes from the Latin word for cattle (*pecus*). Cattle were used to pay for goods and services during the not so distant past. It must have been difficult herding bovines, let alone making sure that they were not BSE (bovine spongiform encephalopathy) and CJD (Creutzfeldt-Jakob disease) carriers. Even with modern transportation, it is still inconvenient to deliver these animals to the slaughterhouses, as these cattle are not the most cooperative passengers.

The currency we use today is not precious metals, mainly because of the inconvenience of carrying heavy metals, not to mention our personal safety and the possibility of getting a hernia.

Depending on whom you ask, money is defined in many ways.

"Money is the medium you use to purchase anything you like in life," is the most common answer. It is considered a necessary article to obtain all the items we need. As one respondent said, money is not the most important thing; it is the only thing. That's a borrowed quotation for sure.

Money is a gauge of wealth. The quantity one owns is used to compute the degree of affluence for an individual or a family.

Money is the gauge of success. Talents' best yardstick of achievement is the amount of money they amassed through the years. Thespians of yesteryears have not lost their magic touch but have been abandoned by their audience. Hench the absence of revenue from their performances.

Money is the root of all evil. This the most common answer by people who are perennially broke. They are advising you to rid yourself of your wicked and sinful possessions. They are willing and happy to unload the burden on your shoulder.

Money makes the world go round. Tevye, a character in *Fiddler on the Roof,* during his conversation with God, asked what is wrong with him having some money. It would allow him to sit all day in the synagogue. He reasoned that people would go to him for advice because rich people have answers to anything, to the dismay of the rabbi.

Whatever your definition of money is, it is important to note that money is nothing but a medium of exchange for goods and services designed for our convenience.

Therefore, the first step to have sufficient cash to buy all the things you want is to understand the following interrelationship.

The Formula for Money Cycle

A crisp Canadian one-hundred-dollar bill may not be acceptable to the merchants of Venice or to the gentlemen peddlers of Verona because they may not know the official exchange rate or the monetary value. They are aware, however, that it is not readily acceptable in the whole of Italy, let alone Europe.

It is important to note that a foreign currency is not acceptable due to the fact that people do not know the value the legal tender represents.

Everyone in the United States knows that five dollars could buy a Big Mac hamburger on sale at McDonald's or that fifteen dollars could pay for a haircut. But a street vendor in Bangkok prefers to deal with Baht because this is their currency in circulation.

Everybody is familiar with the kind of money used in their own country. They think of foreign currencies as fancy pieces of cloth (not paper) with pictures of other national heroes with seemingly inconsequential contributions. Unless, of course, you are Thomas

Cook, dean emeritus of money changers, then it is your job to appreciate the value of any legal tender!

Money per se is just a worthless piece of cloth until a country accepts it as a metric for the value of goods and services, as a means of payment, and as a medium of exchange.

The value of any currency is determined by a complicated formula based on variables such as the GDP, futures market, and the like. This book is concerned only with the value of money and what it represents. The conversion rate to other currencies is not of our immediate interest!

Money is like energy. It cannot be created or destroyed. It can only be converted!

Therefore, the only sensible thing to do is to work on money's equivalent: goods and services. We can create marketable goods and perform desirable services. The three are interrelated.

The following diagram illustrates the conversion cycle of money.

The Conversion Cycle

"The Timeless Formula"

Services (S) <==>Money (M) <==>Goods (G)

Figure 2

The preceding equation (figure 2) with the bidirectional arrows tell us that the triumvirate of money, goods, and services are equal and convertible because they could transform from one form to the other, as long as the values of the goods and services are even to the numerical value printed on the currency. It is also true that any of the trio can be increased, decreased, or remain steady as we please. Money however, cannot be easily increased in value unless we perform services, vend goods, or are doing investments (which is beyond the scope of this book).

Since wealth accumulation is the goal of this book, the above formula can only be accomplished by the buildup of our services or expansion of our inventory of salable goods. Bill Gates provided an operating system called Windows. Jeff Bezos, on the other hand, opened his internet distribution door, which he filled with a plethora of product he christened "Amazon." Like his namesake in the Brazilian forest, the gargantuan outlet is full of items ordered and delivered via couriers.

Our ingenuity, therefore, must be used to manufacture usable goods and to render desirable services. Money is like an empty house. The dwelling has no value until somebody desires to use it for his or her own home; only then does it become a valued asset. Likewise, if a house is valued and sold for $300,000 (US), it is because the buyer knows that he or she could take his or her money by selling it and use the proceeds to purchase other goods and services worth that amount.

We all know that the reward for printing your own money is a long vacation in the big house with an exclusive membership in the club of the rich and infamous. Counterfeiting is not allowed because you did not give back the equivalent value of goods and services!

By the magic of your personal printing press, you increase the count of money in circulation without the equivalent goods and services, which the government refers to as the gross domestic product (GDP).

That is why it is not allowed by law because there was no accounting of the corresponding goods or services.

When the government prints money without the necessary increase in GDP, they devalue the currency in circulation, which causes inflation. That's undesirable, but the law allows it.

However, there is no law against creating lawful goods or services. It is recommended. It is encouraged.

Then convert your goods or services into their financial equivalent. The more goods and services you have, the more money you have. It is that simple. That is the capitalistic way.

Let us examine some examples. Mr. Bill Gates and his partner, Paul Allen, created the operating system for the desktop, making them rich beyond imagination. Were Bill and company the smartest men in the world? Maybe, but they were lucky for sure. Mr. Gates must have had a guardian angel who influenced the board of IBM to award the contract to the partner to develop the disk operating system (DOS) of the personal computer, as it was called then.

Mr. Gates was studying at Harvard University at that time, but his business activities were conflicting with his studies, so he gave up school. Besides, he could teach his professors a thing or two about establishing and running a successful business.

The Harvard professors must have been humbled due to their inferior business accomplishments but prided themselves as the mentors. Whatever the case may be, Bill eventually hired a former schoolmate who finished his MBA at Harvard to be the president of his company.

If Money Could Talk

The wizards of IBM did not believe that the desktop would amount to anything substantial other than a temporary fad soon to find itself in the archives of the Smithsonian Institution. Even Bill Gates then believed that a system with 604 kilobytes of memory would be sufficient to run any conceivable program. Little did he know that in today's PC systems, the volume of memory dedicated is not even enough to control the pesky mouse. What does Bill know, anyway? He just happens to be the wealthiest man in the world several years in a row.

Today, people have no choice but to add to Bill's coffers every time they decide to buy a personal computer. Yes, each computer you own must have a licensed operating system that you pay for; imbedded at the retail store, the cost is disguised with your purchase price. You do not buy a copy of the operating system and install it to all your computers. Your PC must come with the prepaid program installed. You can make a recovery copy, but you will not be able to use it with another computer.

Illegal copy makers violating the copyright law are risking their businesses. Software pirates and forgers are foiled by the incessant effort of big brother Bill to prevent them from an unauthorized peek at his Windows or a view at his Vista's internal functionality.

What is the moral lesson to all this? It is the full understanding that if you want to have money, regardless of the amount, you must give back the corresponding value of goods and services.

The majority of the population is of the mistaken belief that the fastest way to amass money is by betting on the government-sponsored lottery. The lottery is the greatest dream provider. Regardless of the difficulties you are experiencing, there is always the hope that one day you will hit the big one. Why not? A fellow countryman won, and your touch is more magical.

When the going gets tough, the lotto, Powerball, 6/49, and so on provide the hope. The favorite pastime of many people, lottery has been the source of financial dreams. People imagine themselves to be in the winners' circle receiving the coveted check with at least six zeros, smiling at the television camera for their friends to drool and wet themselves with envy.

As stated in this book many times, we must give the equivalent goods and services. Betting on the lottery gives a very high return on an investment! But the possibility of winning is so slim that pundits love to say that you have a better chance of being hit by lightning than of winning the big prize.

Your chances of surviving a lightning strike are even better than the miseries you encounter when you are a winner. There are plenty of horror stories about them. Like gossip, we love to hear the miseries of people we do not like. Don't we love to see the winner suffer?

Countless legends have been created to enhance our interest to buy. How could you miss those catchy slogans: "A winner never quits"; "A quitter never wins"; "Have you practiced your happy dance?"; and so on.

"I am not going to cry over a few dollars" is the most common justification for buying tickets. Who could resist the soothing thoughts of budgeting the imaginary bonanza or the financial relief it brings? Betting, spread over the landscape, seems harmless to individuals, but collectively it is spreading a disease of relying on hopeless causes. Lottery is a convenient process wherein it is legal to steal from one another. Sort of like Robin Hood of Sherwood Forest.

A million dollars in return for few dollars' worth of investment is fantastic indeed. Just look at the queue the next time there is a huge prize.

Hoping for a fairy godmother to bless us with her magic wand is a very slim possibility. So many of us are asking the same favor. It is far easier and maybe more fun to earn the money yourself. With the lessons you will learn from this book, your odds will get better.

Sources of Money

Since money cannot be created, and we cannot print our own, somebody must give it to us legally and willingly in return for the goods we deliver or services we render. But if you must borrow from someone, it must be paid back. Therefore it is best to secure loans from pessimists; they don't expect it back.

It must be fully understood that money, like rivers, has many sources. There are numerous tributaries that make up the mighty Amazon. In the same manner, Amazon.com is made up of a multitude of products. The downside is that this encourages dissatisfaction for a variety of reasons, which reminds us of a man who boycotted every company whose products he cannot afford.

Who is willing to give us money?

People willing to give us money are the recipients of the goods or services we offer in return. This could be anyone. The important thing to remember is that there must a fair exchange.

Therefore let us provide services or goods that keep on giving us an endless supply of what they term in the USA the "green stuff."

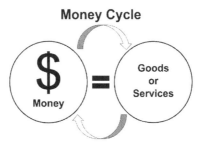

Figure 3

The graphic in figure 3 illustrates the flow of money, goods, and services.

Before money can be earned, we must first decide on a product to manufacture or a service to offer. Then we look for buyers or users who are willing to buy the goods and services we are offering. This is the complete money cycle as seen in the diagram above.

The top arrow illustrates the process of spending your cash, which is the preoccupation of the majority of us. It provides pleasure to our prodigal kin and a nightmare to the spendthrift.

It should be obvious then that the bottom arrow is the best solution when you want to accomplish the reverse (how to earn money). This is the bulletproof evidence of our argument about the production of currency. Simply reverse the process. Voila! You have it! That is simple and straightforward. Now, let us explore the following.

Sources of Income

For this book, we shall discuss the three most popular methods of deriving an income and their proportion in relation to the overall population.

Investors could be either businesspeople or employees. As we said before, investments are not covered in this book, so we will include them but not discuss their participation. For our purposes, it is not necessary to assign an arbitrary percentage. Those who are self-employed could belong in either of the two classifications.

Income Source 1: Employment

The backbone of the industrialized world is employees. There is nothing wrong about remaining an employee for the rest of your life; it's just the inflexibility of adjusting your income at will. The exception is when you are in a high position with a high salary; then the incentive to change might not be an attractive option. If you are happy with your remuneration as an employee, we are happy for you.

Like the proportion in the troika of civilization, analyzing the employee/employer ratio and proportion, the top 5 percent are the employers of the rest. It makes sense because society insidiously designs the system to limit the number of the ruling elite. The top people of the pyramid are coincidentally the employers for the rest.

In any capitalistic society, membership to the other group of workers, white or blue collar, is automatic, and, according to socialists, is a birthright for all of us. The healthy percentage is up to 95 percent for the employees and unemployed (reserve employees). This segment of the population makes their money from remunerations. Note that this percentage varies from one country to another.

This ratio and proportion have been the same arrangement since the beginning of time to the present-day space age. Humankind had changed many things in the field of machineries, equipments, medicine, and sciences, but this numerical balance between employee and employer will likely remain until the end of time.

The civilized world has been in conflict between employees and employers. The same holds true with the military organizational structures, from their highest military rank to the foot soldier, from company chairman of the board to the laborers.

Business, like the military, has commissioned officers that are vastly outnumbered by the private soldiers. Business has to have the same rank and file. There are businesspeople (employers) and workers (employees).

The function of this book is not to criticize this time-tested and internationally accepted norm of ratio and proportion. The primary aim is to understand the structure of civilization and to understand that if anyone of the group wants to transition from employment to business, this person must know what to do. Most especially, you will be made aware of the rules, regulations, and limitations. Later in this chapter, a section deals with monetary influences.

In a communist country, the entire population, except for a few, works for the government, at least in theory. This book is not intended to discuss the merits of communism versus capitalism. Unless we are intending to immigrate to Cuba, Bulgaria, China, or Vietnam, we have to understand that we live in a society where businesses are mostly controlled by the private sector.

It is therefore necessary to understand that the vast majority of the population must work for the businesspeople and entrepreneurs. Society has been structured that way perhaps out of necessity to maintain world order and so forth.

Whatever the rationale, this system has proven to be the most acceptable and is mainly peaceful. There are occasional protests and strikes but nothing that a few canisters of tear gas by a phalanx of overzealous police officers cannot fix and handle.

Employer/Employee Distribution

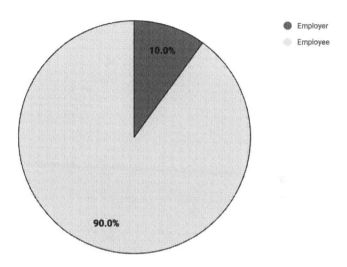

Figure 4

For this illustration, we purposely increased the pie chart between employee and employer to 10 percent. As you can see, the disparity is still wide.

Employment is and will continue to be the dominant method of earning a living. Mark Twain would probably have said, "God must love this group. Why did he make them the majority?"

Unless you are a businessperson or investor, or are self-employed, you must work for somebody to earn a living regardless of your chosen profession. Somebody must utilize your services, and you must be willing to offer it to them.

The charges to customers for the services rendered or the manufacture of goods are not directly proportional to the wages paid to employees. It is also dependent on the employer's willingness to use your services and at what price to meet your terms.

Service/Wages Relationship

Wages are paid based on the agreed amount, deductions and frequency. The employer sets the working conditions, and workers must abide by the covenants of employment agreement or the CBA (collective bargaining agreement), if any.

The employer establishes the wages (payments for services), and employees must agree with the rates set, otherwise employment is not consummated. The bottom line of services as a source of income is the issue of productivity. All works performed have a set value thereby, and the allocated cost cannot exceed the set limit.

For example, if the cost to manufacture a gadget is fifty dollars and takes one hour to manufacture, the maximum labor budget cannot be over that amount regardless of the number of personnel involved in the process or delaying tactics used.

Who Determines What You Earn?

The conventional belief among people is that employees determine how much they are worth. While it is true that in a democratic country you are not forced to do anything against your will, it is wishful thinking to believe that you can dictate how much you can earn. That is the employer's prerogative to agree with your demands; otherwise there is no meeting of the minds.

In the same manner, even a businessperson cannot dictate the income he or she could make. That decision rests in the hands of the customers.

Since the employee is not obligated to accept any job, at any wage, and must agree to all the terms of the job offer, the traditional belief is that "I am in control."

While it is true that there has to be mutual consent, you cannot dictate your salary unless you are in a position of trust. Even then, the issue always boils down to affordability. Otherwise, it is like the favorite expression of US president Donald Trump, "You're fired."

Many of us immigrate to other countries to seek our fame and fortune. Sometimes we do well; the other times it is not what we expect it to be, causing frustrations and resentments.

The Case of the Frustrated Immigrant

Immigrants who have attained a high degree of education find out soon enough that their new country does not recognize the bachelor's degree, master's degree, and the professional designations previously bestowed to them. This is the cause of their frustrations, not realizing that even in their native lands, the titles earned elsewhere are not necessarily recognized either. The following illustrates the case.

Sanjay Mendoza is a gynecologist in his birth country of Sri Lanka. On the strength of his professional qualification, he got accepted to immigrate to Canada. What he did not realize was that he cannot practice his profession in Ontario unless he can successfully secure a Canadian license by OMA (Ontario Medical Association). The effects of a minus-fifteen–degree Celsius temperature and a wind chill factor of minus thirty did not dampen the family's excitement to immigrate.

Toronto is a safe and clean city, they were told. Upon issuance of an immigrant visa, Sanjay and his family sold everything they owned and flew to Toronto in the middle of January, where he expected to practice his profession shortly after arrival. The family's excitement quickly melted like snow in mid-August as soon as he learned of the requirements for a medical doctor's license. The vicarious pain of labor crept through his body, and he wanted to scream at the frustration he felt, thinking that the whole thing was a nightmare. Why? He could deliver triplets with one hand tied behind his back, he wanted to scream at the top of his lungs.

Professional designations such as CA, MD, RN, MBA, LLB, and so forth are the incontestable bailiwick of the regulatory government branch or different colleges who are appointed quasi-governmental bodies that regulate the issuance of licenses. In most cases, there is no outright reciprocity with other countries. The minimum requirement is to pass the rigorous local examination, assuming the college accepts your academic records and a valid license from your own country. The requirements change every now and then.

Sanjay was forced to deliver passengers in a taxicab instead of babies in a hospital. He missed his lucrative practice back home and the comfort of having domestic helpers. He appeared like a deposed emperor without a kingdom or felt exiled. While lining up for passenger pickup, he talked to his fellow drivers registering the same rhetorical complaints. His wife was not only commiserating but on occasion would lead the cries of nostalgia. A friend suggested he should get out of the rut he was in. He replied, "And get out of the delivery business."

The children, on the other hand, loved the adopted country. The Canadian school system was more to their academic taste. The offspring were not ready to pack and set foot to the past. Besides, it was embarrassing to return and admit failure.

So with so much regret, the family braved the harsh winter with the ardent hope that spring would bring a fresh set of expectations along with the blooming tulips and chirping birds of summer.

The year 2008 will be remembered as one of the worst recessions in history. It was global in scope and was severe. Large companies declared bankruptcy or were at the brink of falling into the abyss. Gasoline prices were at an all-time high. The conversations around the water coolers of most offices were about how to save on rising transportation costs.

"The magnitude of your income determines your value to the community."

That is a loaded statement. How can your income have any bearing on your importance to society? How can you equate your financial worth to your value to the community?

Indeed, you can. The person who provides the most goods and services will earn the most money. Therefore that person is very important to the community. It is that simple.

Sam Walton with his Walmart stores all over the continent made his heirs billionaires because they supply many household goods. The same is true with Amazon.

The merchants, the entrepreneurs, the professionals, and key employees attract the best compensations. It is the law of nature that these people get to sit on a pedestal, their pocketbooks lined with money, and command the most respect!

The Land of Milk and Honey

The intellectual savviness of people from economically depressed areas dictates that they should abandon their domicile in favor of a greener pasture regardless of the hazards of an arduous journey. Countries such as India, Vietnam, and the Philippines, who desperately wanted the foreign invaders to give them independence, are now taking chances by illegally immigrating to the country of their so-called invaders.

Why do people have to brave the harsh Sonoran Desert, fight the deadly ocean waves of the Caribbean Sea in a makeshift boat, or try to cross the Pacific in rusty, overloaded container vessels?

If one survives the close perils of the ocean and the border patrols, the immigration officers are even more difficult to deal with than the tsunami waves of the seas. The welcome mat laid at the front door of detention centers and interview rooms is not for prospective employers but for police officers and judges.

What prompted those daring adventurers who take these perilous voyages? It is with the mistaken belief that the meadows are more robust on the other side of the ocean. Even if this is true, the price to pay for the benefits is like what King Pyrrhus said in his victory speech against the Romans: "If we keep winning, there will be nobody left." A Pyrrhic victory indeed, the adjective coined in his honor.

Your personal mother lode could be located right in your own backyard. All you have to do is get the appropriate picks and shovels and commence to dig. Your geographical odds are greatly enhanced if your residence is in Gotland, Sweden, where legends believe that buried treasures are everywhere.

The Reckoning

The topic of conversation during the fourth quarter of 2008 was job security. Everyone knew somebody who had lost his or her job. Many people have lost their savings, their homes, and their dreams of a prosperous lifestyle. Company presidents were willing to work with one dollar per year of compensation with the hope that the future will be better.

Most of these magnates probably have money saved up to cushion them on the rainy days, unlike the rest of us—most of whom do not have funds to take the slack for a week, let alone years. Many employees have difficulty transitioning to new jobs.

First, they will insist on a salary equal to if not better than their old jobs. A displaced manager will insist on being given the same position and salary from a new employer. It is not acceptable to step down from a prestigious position, and the new employer must maintain the old standard of living these displaced employees used to have.

Second, one must understand that one's employment could be terminated for reasons of obsolescence. Technologies, contrary to popular belief, do not eliminate jobs. They simply change the qualifications of the employees. These employees have to be retrained, or they are eliminated. Postal workers are examples. They used to sort mail by hand. The only skill needed was the ability to read and throw the mail into the appropriate pigeon slot.

Then automation entered the picture. The mail-sorting technology had been introduced, requiring workers to use a keyboard to input postal codes. They had to learn keyboarding skills with acceptable speed, dexterity, and accuracy. New employees were added; some were left behind to service customers who refused to adapt to the new mailing procedure.

If the need for your skills has joined the fate of the dodo bird, your best bet is to acquire a new marketable skill.

When is the best time to look for a new employer? The answer to this is when you have a job. In a section on business management in chapter 2, you will learn that the function of an employer is to recruit, train, and retain employees. For this reason, it is in the best interest of businesspeople to prevent you from applying for another job. These employers will meet demands if you have a diplomatic approach.

But there are so many downsides to searching for a job when you do not have one. The feeling of desperation is difficult to conceal; therefore, your bargaining position is compromised. Besides, you are inclined to accept the first opportunity that comes your way.

Many businesspeople are involved in more than one business. This is in preparation for slowdowns, threats of competition, or simple obsolescence, as stated previously. The adrenalin rush for a businessperson is the challenge of embarking on a new venture. It is inconceivable that Bill Gates or Warren Buffet will ever stop. After all, making deals are the activities a seasoned businessperson cannot pass up.

Income Source 2: Business

Securing admittance into this fraternity and sorority of exclusive people is both straightforward and difficult. It is simple because to gain acceptance you do not have to be scrutinized by a discriminating panel of interviewers probing your every intention, background, and reputation. In fact, if there is a group, they probably will dissuade you from joining. The reality of it is that we do not even go far beyond our self-imposed restriction. We throw in the towel long before we attempt to gain admission.

The decision to become a businessperson is as terrifying as skydiving for a person with acrophobia. The jungle we are about to enter is infested with unknown creatures ready to scare us to death simply because we are unfamiliar with the terrain and do not know what to do.

The difficulty and complexity of business as a source of money can be demonstrated in the following farm story.

The hog in a farm tried to convince the chicken that the only way they could be free from the confines of a captive environment was to go into business themselves. The chicken refused.

The hog said, "It is easy for you to decide; you will only be involved, while I will be committed. It is better to be a living disappointment than a departed subject!"

That in a nutshell explains why only 10 percent, the maximum number of people, go into business.

Employment is involvement; business is a commitment.

As employees, our involvement in the operation of a business is limited. Employees render the required hours of work, perform specific assigned jobs, and then are free to get on with their personal lives. That is involvement.

The business owner, on the other hand, cannot just switch off his or her mind from his or her business. He or she thinks of the events of the day (e.g., the sales/marketing activities, productions, accounting, and managing people). He or she plans for the following day's challenges and for how to avoid potential problems.

If things are not under control, the business owner could lose more than cash and shirt. Everything must work. There are many things at stake. That is commitment.

Since the business owner has the lion's share of the responsibilities and losses if there is a failure, it is reasonable to expect that he or she will reap the majority of the sweet reward of conquest.

We all want to be rich; *ipso facto*, we must all be in business. We can then live in the lap of luxury and savor the lifestyle of the rich and famous. We live in a country where we are free to choose, do whatever we please—with some restriction, of course—and as Robin Leach would say, "have champagne wishes and caviar dreams." What a fantasy world that would be—Utopia on earth; we all can take that. But hold on! If all of us are in business, then who are going to be our employees? If all of us are playing chiefs, who is going to set up our teepees and fight our tribal conflicts?

If the entrepreneurial bug infested the brains of many citizens of the industrialized world, we would run out of employees. Maybe that is why illegal immigrants are tacitly allowed in addition to legitimate ones. The legal process of immigration is too slow to keep up with the demands of labor.

Depending on your country and on who to believe, less than 10 percent of the population own and control about 85 percent of the nation's wealth, as we said in the introduction. These figures vary constantly, depending on how many of the population get smart enough to change to a better economic class.

The choice should be easy to make. If you want to be in the top of society, then go into business. Chapter 3 discusses the advantages of going into business. This book is not able to give you all the details of how to start a business but will cover the basics. Here are some things to consider.

Business Vs. Employment

Business: The buck stops with you!
Employment: The buck is paid to you!

Business: There are clients that are sadistic!

Employment: They are your supervisors!

Business: You do not want the time to end, especially with deadlines!
Employment: You cannot wait for the time to end!

Business: You have to pay employees and suppliers regularly!
Employment: You expect to be paid regularly!

Business: You worry about your business when on vacation!
Employment: You get paid to go on vacation!

Business: You get headaches from nonpaying customers!
Employment: You get headaches from nonpaying employers!

Business: You thrive on responsibility!
Employment: You avoid responsibility!

Business: Lack of sales is disastrous!
Employment: Lack of sales signals vacation time!

Business: Procrastination is lost opportunity!
Employment: Procrastination is job security!

Business: Customer satisfaction is job one!
Employment: Customer satisfaction is one more job!

Business: Irreplaceable you!
Employment: Replaceable you!

Business: Success is its own reward!
Employment: Success is somebody's reward!

Business: You plan not to fail!
Employment: You fail to plan!

Business: You look after number one!
Employment: You look for number one!

Income Source 3: Self-Employment

To be employed is to have an employer, while being in business means you employ and manage people.

Self-employment is both. Like the larvae of the entomological world, the insects had metamorphosed into larva but declined to complete the process by emerging as a butterfly. They are the Joeys of the business outback. The marsupial pouch is comfortable, safe, and well served. Why would anyone venture into the unknown?

Likewise, self-employment is like a baby who refuses to complete the gestation period. This person cannot adhere to the rigid rules of the workplace but is not ready to take the full thrust and responsibilities of a complete businessperson—meaning to have employees and, if they do, only a very limited number, such as secretaries. Like the anecdote in the business section of the chicken and the hog, he or she cannot decide to play foul or hogwash.

Being self-employed is like Jackie Mason in his Tony Award acceptance speech for *The Jackie Mason Show*; he had no one to thank because he was the producer, the director, and the actor. He was everything.

Are they narcissistic or incapable of trusting someone? Who knows? On the bright side, it is difficult to argue or fight with yourself. This is for peaceful coexistence, supposedly.

This is the Shangri-La of the employment world.

Income Source 4: Investment

This is not a book about investments. The reason is because investments rely heavily on capital! Accumulating capital is one of the main objectives of this book. Therefore, you have to learn first the best way to earn money, have enough to spend for yourself, and then invest the remainder.

There are hundreds if not thousands of books already written on the subject! Pick the one appropriate for you and have fun; we wish you plenty of luck.

The mandate of this book is to assist the reader in earning money in return for goods and services. Whether you spend the money you earn or invest, it is yours to decide.

All roads may lead to Rome, but not all investments return with interests, compounded or not. Sometimes, you are lucky if you recoup your original capital.

In the year 2008, billions of dollars in savings were blown away like dust in the open air! One wonders if saving or investing for a rainy day makes sense anymore. Our appointed caretakers for our wealth are like arsonists given the responsibility of safeguarding our piles of paper assets from fire. The thief is our chief of police.

Ebert of WorldCom, Kowalski of Tyco, Skilling of Enron, Black of Hollinger, John and Timothy Rigas of Adelphia, and so on have gone to prison serving terms for crimes against stockholders. While these offenders serve in the penitentiary, people who lost in their stocks and savings are still licking their financial wounds.

One wonders where Ken Lay ended up—heaven or hell. If he ended up in hell, we are sure Ken can call on his former friends from Houston to extinguish the flame; after all, they are expert firefighters.

In reality, all employees with pension plans are investors through the investment pools of their pension plans. The Canada Pension Plan (CPP), to which all working Canadians are required to contribute, have their contributions invested in select companies allowed by law.

If that government pension plan holds some Microsoft stocks, they can think of themselves as business partners of Bill Gates and Paul Allen, but they never get to be invited to the shareholders' meeting, let alone to have a lunch date with them.

The Monetary Influences

As you have seen previously, there are several ways of earning money. Who has influenced and steered us to follow a specific direction?

More importantly, why is it so difficult to break free from the yellow brick road of life? Why can we not just program our modus operandi of earning money like we do with our GPS? We briefly touch on the subject about our affinity to paychecks in other sections of this book. Here we look at it in more detail.

In real life, there are few things that are easy to give up. We hang on to them like an infant clinging to his baby bottle, but if addiction is added to the equation, no amount of methadone can free us from the chemical bondage. Worse, we do not even acknowledge the cerebrally embedded reliance on the unproductive practice.

Like any dependency, we are fixated on the unwavering regularity of its arrival. It comes in a variety of ways—check via mail, direct deposit, or simply outright cash. We depend on it so much that if it is delayed, the withdrawal symptoms cannot be camouflaged due to the brewing panic attack.

If we know the contributing factors, perhaps we could abate their influences, if we chose to do so. How could we ligate ourselves from the nutritional therapy of perennial financial inadequacies and for once enjoy the luxury of abundance? Who are the obstructionists lining up life's hurdles?

Parents

Parents have the most profound influence when it comes to the shape of our personalities. Our minds, both conscious and subconscious, are nourished with positive or negative thoughts. Our parents, being the first people we saw and lived with, can implant prosperity consciousness, affluence as well as poverty.

The saying "tell me who your friends are, and I will tell you who you are" is not entirely accurate because the ones with the most influence on your character, through genetics, are your parents. You are like your parents not your friends. We even look like them in appearance. Upon adulthood, we find ourselves emulating our parents' temperaments and characters automatically.

Many children rebel against their closest relatives, as in the case of Michael Douglas, who in the end stepped into the footsteps of his father and was an equally good actor like Kirk Douglas. Kirk said in his acceptance of his honorary Oscar lifetime achievement award that if he knew that his son Michael would be such a phenomenal success, he would have been nicer to him.

With all due respect, this book is not intended to criticize our parents. There is no effort to belittle the difficult task of rearing children. We have great admiration and love for our parents for being there when we needed them the most. The moment we were born until we have our first jobs, our parents supplied us with all our financial needs without expectation of payments. They gave us their best. They bent over backward to make us happy with exotic toys, designer clothes, bicycles, cars, college education, and whatever we were able to convince our parents to buy for us.

Our parents may have unwittingly trained us to rely on handouts for the rest of our lives. We become addicted to the practice of allowing others to do our thinking and be our support. Parents do not demand payments for all the things they have done for their children. As a result, there are some adults who cannot afford or are unwilling to be weaned from the bosoms of their parents. The invisible umbilical cord clings tightly like Gorilla Glue. It is challenging to give up "on demand" financial assistance.

A mother complained one day that her son was not concerned at all about his future. The father wisely remarked, "Why should he? You are doing all the worrying for him."

If you are from the lucky gene society, you probably learn at an early age the theory of *quid pro quo*, or that everything has a price. This could be the most important lesson you learned from Mom and Dad, especially the principle of reciprocity in finances. "I let my children earn their allowances," said a martinet father. This is not to put them in the mutuality grind but to let them appreciate and groove in the spirit of give and take.

The point at issue is that we metamorphose to adulthood and assume grown-up responsibilities. While it is fun taking care of our children, it is not pleasant to do the same thing to a person of age, irrespective of his or her household chore-handling brilliance. Like all good things, it must come to the departure terminal of life. Your bags must be packed, and you get ready to go. What an ending it would be if you are unprepared to construct and maintain your domestic rampart.

Our parents are supposed to catechize us about domiciliary chores. But how can they do an excellent job when the offspring are constantly worried about where the next family meal will come from? It is worse if they are the nemesis of the bill collectors.

Here is a story to illustrate the point as related by a businessperson.

A twelve-year-old boy approached me while filling up my car in a self-serve gas bar and offered to do the service for me. I politely declined. This boy asked if he could wash my windshield. Again, I refused his offer. Finally, out of desperation, he offered to sing a song for me. By then, I had filled up my car and instead offered to give him the loose change I had in my pocket.

The boy said, "Thank you, but I cannot accept because you won't let me do anything for you."

If this boy learned that lesson from his parents, they deserve a medal of honor. They deserve to be placed on a pedestal for a job well done.

The problem of unemployment is severe, especially in third world countries. The majority of the population is unskilled. People in this situation do not understand the principle of paying a fee for all services or goods or vice versa.

The expectation is that an employer must set up and run a business that fits the prospective employee's skills and preferences.

This is worse than a domestic helper dictating to the house owner what appliances he or she can buy or what business to be in. This person acts as if he has taken over from St. Peter his responsibilities as gatekeeper of the Pearly Gates.

The School System

The next group of people to have direct influence over our economic minds are the institutions we attended to further our educational developments. These are the educators entrusted with the pedagogical training to shape our minds to be productive members of our community. However, there are society red lines that we must not cross lest we disturb the imposed balance. If you think this demarcation was written with disappearing ink, think again because there are inconspicuous enforcers on the lookout to steer you in the right direction.

These teachers are the indispensable dramatis personae for our success, especially at the higher levels of education such as master's and doctorate degrees. The founders of Google and Yahoo started developing their business ideas during their graduate academic years.

All successful activities can only be accomplished with thorough knowledge about the subjects we deal with in employment or business. The school system will help us understand the theories to use and give us the initial theoretical experience.

Though the school assumptions may vary from work application, it will give us the theoretical understandings of the real McCoys. The lessons are practice runs while you are dealing with Monopoly money. The only thing that could get hurt is our pride, which is probably the only thing we can swallow without adding to our waistline. Should we eat crow, the resulting pain is benign.

The paramount advantage of the school system is as an adjunct to our pride and narcissistic egos, a very important ingredient to our wills to succeed. You would be hard-pressed to find a master of business administration (MBA), especially from any Ivy League school, whose self-esteem is not running on full throttle. The sheepskin diploma effects are not only on our knowledge and abilities but also on the dignity and self-confidence. You cannot put a price on the latter.

The school system has flaws. One of the mistakes can be traced to the preuniversity guidance counselors. They are entrusted to guide the innocent students to the royal road of a promising future, yet the counselors may be struggling financially themselves, a case of the sightless leading the visionless.

Another egregious blunder is the idea of associating the course to take with the subjects in which the student did well during his or her lower academic years. The prospective course's possible earning potential should be commensurate to the lifestyle the student wishes to have.

Let us take the case of a student who loves to study anatomy and is interested in the yin and yang of the human body. He goes on to study acupuncture thinking that he could help people get rid of their aches and pains and earn enough money to have a good life. What he does not realize is that no matter how many needles he introduces in the epidermis and no matter how much he practices his craft, he cannot earn beyond "pin money," as they say in the pricking business.

For example, if the student wants an income of $1 million per annum in 2020, upon graduation to maintain his intended lifestyle, a course in engineering may not design it, regardless of how accurate he is in mathematics. Even If he has an edge in computer-aided design! It does not add up. His slide rule will not point to the right answer. This is true unless the student intends to use his academic training as a business base for his great engineering ideas, such as designing and marketing a new vacuum cleaner that revolutionizes the sanitation process to make a financial cleanup of the marketplace. This way, the student did not waste his time with his education, and his great electrical ideas did not simply get sucked up and gather dust.

First, the financial goal must be specified. How much money will the student require to adequately meet his prospective modus vivendi? Then the student must fit the course to the level of income required, regardless of his academic interest. This is putting the horse before the cart.

Look at the curriculum of any university. These institutions offer hundreds of courses designed to produce professionals: secretaries, engineers, lawyers, and doctors, for example. Regardless of the course a student takes, there is only one goal. It is limited to teaching the students enough knowledge for employment. It is up to the student to transform that knowledge into a marketable skill to maximize earning potential. Lawyers, accountants, and medical doctors could earn enough money by becoming self-employed so their incomes could be flexible.

The graduate, if lucky enough to find a job immediately, will realize right away whether the time spent in school was worth every cent of the tuition or was a complete waste of time. Some will have regrets, while others will be celebrating.

For the remorseful group, they will conclude that they took the wrong course because there is no demand for their skills or the earnings are too low to live on the living standard they were hoping for. Where did these students go wrong?

Colleges and universities are excellent places to learn skills and the know-how to apply them. The training you receive is geared toward a career as an employee or, at the very best, self-employment.

We flock to seminars conducted by presumably successful people with the hope that their talismans would rub on us and lead us to our pot of gold. Wisely or foolishly, we spend thousands of dollars buying their books and tapes to add to our collections of dust gatherers. At least, the decision came from us.

Government

The first order of the government is to maintain peace and order. The tacit solution to this dilemma is to create different social holding cells to contain the different strata of society. It is difficult to ascertain how the authorities sorted the selection of original members for each group, whether voluntary selection or enforced membership, it is hard to determine.

The job of politicians is a thankless one. They are leading a country with three different groups of people as described in the introduction. The equilibrium must be maintained at all times with the assistance of the school system. As if there is an imaginary military police officers who will steer stray cattle back into the herd. It is difficult to break free unless you have the firm determination to dissociate yourself from the cohesive flock. The empty space provided by the formation of migrating birds makes you fly with ease so that you can get addicted to the privilege. You conclude that it is best to tow the line.

People will always follow the path of least resistance. That is the law of nature. Politicians, in order to get elected, will promise anything to get your votes; these authorities are subservient to the foibles of their subjects. If you have weak knees, the government will not encourage you to walk and exercise but to just take it easy and relax. "We will take care of you," is the advice.

For those who are iconoclast, you are a step ahead of the society's demarcation line. You are used to going against the flow, an important characteristic for making changes. All you have to do is to educate yourselves from obscurity to prosperity? The answer to the above is coming up.

Our Own Research

Before the industrial revolution, there were few books to read, and they were scarcely available. Great inventors like Edison and Bell had to discover most of the theories and concepts of their projects. They did things by trial, error, and success. These assumptions had been revised many times over.

When Henry Ford patented the automobile combustion engine, it is doubtful if he had all the books on the science of engines. The same is true with Tesla, who discovered the alternating current (AC) in competition squarely to Thomas Edison, who favored direct current (DC). Tesla was the father of alternating current, and he may have written the books on that subject. Why not? He was the undisputed expert at that time.

At the advent of the industrial revolution, processes had to be formulated by management and owners such as the assembly line method of manufacturing started by Henry Ford. New equipment required new discoveries.

The idea of making personal discoveries is referred to as doing your own research.

From Other People

There are times that books are not sufficient for our needs. In that case, we may have to experiment on our own. All other lessons have to be experimented or learned. If we need someone to help and guide us in understanding the application of complex mathematical formulae, we may consult professionals who are experts in that field.

It is preferable to be under the tutelage of a reliable mentor in the art of deduction. Learning becomes easier when you have someone to bounce ideas off of. Many great minds have apprenticed under a master who was then able to refine their crude ways.

Successful parents can influence their children to be victorious and prosperous by being an example. This is due in part to the ingrained, acquired, or congenital belief that fortune favors those who have reserved a seat to be on top of the heap.

With the multitude of ways of reaching and touching someone, there is no excuse of not communicating with others. We can fax, email, video chat, or the old-fashioned way of writing via mail.

From Books/Internet

A visit to the library used to be the obvious first step in gathering information regarding our business projects and plans. At the outset, we have a plethora of questions that need to be answered.

Now, all of us, even kids, are equipped with a portable device hooked online ready to provide the clarifications of our most complex inquiry. This method of data gathering gave new meaning to the phrase "let your fingers do the walking."

For the sake of convenience, we have a choice of typing the question or simply verbally dictate our query, and the response is instantaneously displayed in the screen.

Knowledge—Conclusion

The main objective of life from birth to death is the acquisition of knowledge. It is ironic that the human race has to learn most of the skills needed for our lives. Some lessons are instinctive like the feeding reflex, but the majority have to be learned. These wisdoms have to come from somewhere or somebody. Initially we just imbibe them unflinchingly until we reach the age of reason, or have enough reservoir of knowledge to decipher the veracity of the information passed on.

The paradox of life is that the people who are genuinely interested in our welfare are the ones whose perspicaciousness is highly repugnant to us. The flowchart in the appendix shows a few of the possible paths to follow. Regardless of the path you choose, the starting point is the acquisition of knowledge, be it in school or on your own; without educating yourself, you will not progress in life.

It has been said that knowledge always pays the highest interest and is something that will stay with you forever. People without expertise could not expect to be useful to themselves, let alone others. Yet, they wonder why they are in a permanent state of impecuniousness.

The Side Effects of Welfare

The most counterproductive practice of any government is the welfare system. Money, as we now know, must be earned. There has to be an equitable exchange of goods or services for the benefit we receive. While there are worthy recipients, like the elderly and persons with disabilities and illnesses, others are functional but refuse to carry their own weight.

Some of the welfare recipients are justified morally and legally. This book is not intended to criticize the system but merely to point out that this giveaway program is one of the myriad examples where the fair exchange of goods and services for money is ignored. Lack of control on the part of the government is at fault.

Families on welfare receive money in the mail. They do not have to work for it. They do not have to do anything to deserve it other than being in the right place at the right time. They are just lucky enough to be citizens of a country that can afford to provide such a program. The parents in that group obviously will not teach their children the valuable lesson of give and take for the money they receive. People in this bunch stay in the program for generations.

It is possible that a child influenced by the welfare tradition could not envision himself outside of the entitlement check. These children attribute their substandard lives to bad luck. They have not been educated in the art of earning their own money.

The Bottom Line

Regardless of the profession you are in or how you earn your money, the following illustrates the income and expense flow.

Women would define a successful man as one who earns more money than his wife could spend. Smart is the woman who could lead this money machine to the altar.

This is a case where if the woman has an excellent bottom, all she has to do is snare the man with an excellent bottom line.

The year 2008 was when the global economy went on a tailspin. Individuals and families were afflicted with "deficit-itis." Companies were forced to lay off employees because the corporate income no longer could maintain their payroll.

The most pressing problem of any family in the world, except the wealthy, is AIDS (Acute Income Deficiency Syndrome), which could simply be remedied by MRI (More Revenue and Income).

Countries such as Canada and the United States have budgetary shortfalls because the revenue they have collected is smaller than their expenses. Governments, unlike individuals, have more options to deal with fiscal crises. Government can simply print more money! Families and individuals are not so fortunate. The only beneficiaries are the collection agencies, credit counselors, and bankruptcy courts.

If we cannot restrain our spending, the least we can do is increase our earnings. Our financial programs should be the opposite of our diet agendas. If all our calorie intakes are way more than our usages, the result will be weight gain. If our incomes can outweigh our expenses, then the result will be savings.

Everyone will be in shape and have no financial worry. It is that simple but is not easily attainable.

Ultimate Word

There is a Broadway show titled *The Roar of the Greasepaint—The Smell of the Crowd*, where the title song, sung by Anthony Newley, is "Who Can I Turn To?" and is a classic example. The song by Leslie

Bricusse and Anthony Newley expressed the lesson advocated in this opening chapter: Who can I turn to? They asked the question because the authors knew that if nobody needs them, they have to resort to stealing, borrowing, or begging.

Nobody can articulate the facts of this section any better than the immortal song. It must be the saddest feeling to be unwanted; nobody cares to use your skills—ipso facto, no one is willing to pay for your products and services.

How do you find what you are after? This chapter has shown that money can be earned if money's equivalent is fully understood! Goods when produced and services when rendered can throw away our sorrows, and then we can have our share of laughter.

The flip side of this equation is the unpleasant alternative: beg, steal, or borrow!

Beg: That is exactly what the welfare recipients are doing to the government or to charities. That is precisely the forte of panhandlers. It is inconceivable for any able-bodied human being with a stable mental capacity to resort to a suppliant lifestyle. People, they say, are like electricity; they will follow the path of least problem and care.

Steal: The penitentiary is full of detainees confined for using their ingenuity to purloin the properties of others. The crimes they committed can only be executed with careful planning and coordination. If only it was used to benefit their fellow people.

Borrow: How many relationships—friendly, sanguine, affinity, or business partners—are not on speaking terms anymore due to unpaid debt? Relationships were doing well until debt tore them apart. There is a saying that the fastest way to lose a friend is to lend him or her money.

If money could talk, it would want us to know it better by understanding fully the concepts it epitomizes.

If money could talk, it would tell us that no member of a civilized society in any country is restricted in owning any amount of money as long as it is obtained legally, and taxes are duly paid.

If money could talk, it would warn us that misunderstanding could lead to chaos, jealousy, and discord.

If money could talk, it would tell us that it is only a catalyst and that in reality we should not be thinking about it but concentrating on the equivalent goods and services.

CHAPTER 2

Business Theories

The keen recommendations of the previous chapters are that entrepreneurial activities are excellent and are a very satisfying method of earning money. You have the most control and flexibility to adjust in midstream.

Therefore, if money could talk, it would want us to learn all the intricacies of business. Let us find out why.

The denotation of business is one's work, occupation, or profession that engages a person's time, care, and attention. It is a practice of making one's living by engaging in commerce. For the purposes of our discussion and study, we will stick to this definition.

It implies that it is something we do that requires our time, painstakingly and with a considerable amount of perseverance. It involves the rendering of services or exchange of goods with the end result of earning money. With that as a premise, it would mean that we have to deal with clients and customers. There is an interchange of the commodities involved among people, in the process of which money is expected to follow.

Since business involves the effective and productive use of our time, the amount of time that we put into business is directly proportional to the amount of money earned. We can express that in a corollary thus:

If your business involvement is only part time, you will achieve partial results.

It is encouraging to note that once we have established a well-managed business, we could duplicate ourselves through effective use of delegation, which we will also discuss in more detail in a later chapter. The advantage of duplication is the ability to accomplish more given the same time limitation.

This would mean more time for the family, travel, sports, hobbies, shows, and things that we cannot otherwise do with employment limitations. Consequently, we would lead a more healthy life with the acceptance of stress and workload.

It is easy to say that if you don't have the time, make it. While some people may not feel comfortable about the time they will have to sacrifice in any field of interest, it is said that given the proper incentive, a person would perform well in any endeavor. We can state then that one reason people do not venture into business is the lack of motivation or inadequate understanding of some business philosophies or theories.

Let us examine a few theories with some depth that we will find important in a potential undertaking.

The 3 *W*s of Business

Why?

Why not? Business is a field where the common person fears to tread. Some reasons are understandable but not acceptable once we realize that we are responsible to carve a prosperous and successful life with meaning. We need to believe that we are not a bona fide member of the herd by adhering to the set mentality.

The primary reason people avoid business is apprehension. While we may have the audacity of hope, we cannot erase from our minds the tenacity of fear. We are scared to rock the boat of our smug existence. We are afraid to disturb our comfort zones. We are comfortable in calm, shallow waters, so why risk the dubious steps into the unknown rapids or deeper waters?

It is extremely difficult for the majority to venture into something they are not so familiar with. This is especially true if they realize that they have to give up something of utmost significance in life or if they were asked to put their feeling of employment security on a tightrope, especially when they have a steady job, with earnings sufficiently covering their expenses. Why should they give it up even if what they are about to embark on is a more promising financial prospect? Assuming without necessarily conceding that it could be true, what guarantees do they have? Whatever happened to the saying that a bird in the hand is worth two in the bush?

Chapter 1 recommends that the best method of earning money is to be involved in business, either as a full-time occupation or to augment one's income. The nagging claim that has been proven to be true by empirical observation is this: you cannot become rich unless you get involved with business or become a successful investor or work a high-paying job as an employee.

Let us look at who are the rich people in our communities. They are the inheritors of old money, showbiz people because of their talents and popularity, or businesspeople who are operators of successful ventures. Therefore, if you are not a blessed member of a wealthy family or endowed with exceptional sports or showmanship abilities or other marketable skills, you have to embark on an entrepreneurial activity. Since money is represented by goods and services, and the businesspeople are the producers of them, it is no wonder that if they succeed, they are rewarded immensely. Why is this so?

The most cogent reason for going into business is the duplication factor. To illustrate this theory, let us look at a beehive. There are millions of worker bees doing all the jobs required in the colony, from gathering nectar to repairing the hive and tending for the young. How productive would the hive be if the queen bee had to do all of this work alone? What would happen if there are thousands of beehives to do the soldiering, hive repairs, honey gathering, and egg laying queens? There would be chaos in the blooming forest, for instead of a centralized nesting site, there would be millions of little nests competing for foods, a giant nightmare for the colonies.

Our civilized business society seems to have patterned its structure the same way. We have many protectorates, each with a patriarch, a matriarch, and laborers. There is no impediment to establishing your own outpost unless you have green but arthritic thumbs, have a hemophiliac ego, or simply are content to be a statistic.

Always remember, though, that there is no substitute for healthy competition. The problem arises when people's greed gets the better of them. As we said earlier, the love of money is the root of all evil. You need to understand that in the world of business, if we all play fairly, there are enough slices for everyone. There are many business opportunities around; all you have to do is wake up your wealth accumulation instinct.

While the road to prosperity is paved with good intentions, it is full of frustrated and lonely travelers where only few survive to benefit from their perseverance. Those who survive and live to tell the tale realize this undeniable fact.

While employment is the most convenient method of earning a living, the number one drawback is the limited number of hours we can allocate for work. If our jobs cramp our lifestyles, this is one case where time cannot alleviate or cure the pain!

We all have twenty-four hours a day divided between our jobs and other activities of daily living. Normally, we allocate eight hours for our work and use the remainder for the rest of our concerns. The ratio is constant. Different people have different ways of allocating their time. We need to value it, because as they say, time lost cannot be recovered. If we lose it, we cannot retrieve it. It is gone. It is history. That is why we have to seize the moment. The present is all we have. The poet says, "For yesterday is but a dream, and tomorrow is but a vision." We cannot let time wait in order to accommodate our personal preferences. We cannot stop the world the way we hail a bus.

Not even daylight saving time (DST) can alter the situation. All it does is take advantage of the presence of daylight. The number of hours for the rotation of the earth comes as a natural phenomenon as well as the revolution around the sun, making it constant. It is a physical law that is not open for alteration although some may try in vain.

That is no different from Papito's solution to lengthen his blanket by cutting a section from one end and attaching it to the other.

Some may work double shifts in one day to more than double their pay by virtue of overtime. However, employers know that a person's productivity can only go so far, as it is considerably decreased after eight hours of nonstop work. The setback of this arrangement is the inability to keep working without adequate rest before our bodies yield to fatigue. Like machines, our bodies also need rest as well as recreation to maximize production.

In an attempt to earn more, some employees overdo this, and they earn the moniker OT (overtime) queen or king. The problem arises because the situation could turn extremely dangerous and life threatening, thus jeopardizing the liability of the employing company. It could cause bulging varicose veins, heart conditions, and other health hazards, or sleeping in the subways or while driving home could be a potential cause for theft or fatal accident.

Another option to increase earnings is to negotiate for a pay raise. While this may be necessary and fair to some, this process can turn ugly and cause embarrassment; oftentimes, it leads to hostile feelings between the employer and the employee. One has to understand that in most cases, unless there is a considerable amount of arm-twisting or the boss is overly generous for whatever humanitarian rhyme or reason, the answer to any pay increase demand will likely be negative. It is obvious that any increment increase in anyone's salary could mean a corresponding decrease in the company's profit. The reasons are more exhaustively outlined.

A salary raise means getting more payment without the corresponding increase in productivity. But then, money has to come from somewhere for the employer to afford the raise in labor cost.

The employer either increases the prices of goods and services produced or decreases profits!

Those are the only two options. The size of the cake remains the same no matter how you slice it. The whole is always equal to the sum of its parts. Getting a smaller slice is the last thing the employer wants. It is plain human nature, just as the employee likewise wants more in the tug of war. That situation eventually escalates into a full-blown fertile ground for animosities and sour relationships between the two sides of the equation. This is true unless they come up with a commonly acceptable compromise where everybody is happy, which is rare and far and few between. That explains why there is perennial haggling at the bargaining table.

Salary Raise

The above illustrates the dilemma an employer faces every time a salary increase is implemented. The employee wants to shift his or her financial problems to the employer. Will it be a welcome handover? Don't bet on it. It is a dark horse.

Should the employer increase the prices of goods and services, which will make them less competitive in the marketplace, or settle for decreased profits, which will drive away investors of the company or tighten credit facilities? It is a dilemma wherein there are no easy answers.

If your employer is the government, all they have to do is raise taxes. For private industry, it is not so straightforward. The choice is always between two unfavorable alternatives. There is hardly any chance to take the dilemma bull by the horns.

Regardless of the steps the employer takes, somebody has to bite the bullet. Are there alternatives? Yes, there are, but they may not be pleasantly acceptable to both parties. The smile elicited might be like that of a dental patient on Novocain. Let us examine the other options.

If we want to earn more money, we can negotiate with our own employers to perform additional work.

It is now a matter of the employer deciding whether or not to allow us to perform extra services that mean extra hours for production for you or do the additional work given the same amount of time. Hopefully, our employers need the extra production.

However, if we are ready to make that small step of walking into business and that giant leap into uncertainty, it would be a commendable move because one of the scariest things to do is to transition from a permanent job to full-time business. It could mean a suicidal jump from the frying pan into the fire. To give up the security of a regular paycheck is as scary as jumping into a pool full of water of insecurities, especially when we cannot swim. Here is my own experience.

On the final day of my last job, my friend, a coemployee, came over to congratulate me. Or to be more precise, he came over to make a final attempt to convince me to reverse my decision. He got misted up on the momentous occasion as he intimated to me that he wished he could have made the same move as I did but did not.

I asked him, Why not? He sheepishly admitted that he could not give up the security the government of Canada, our employer, provides. Not to mention that getting into this job itself is an envy to many, as the screening process is stringent. He added that like me, he had young children to feed and educate and outstanding debts like mortgages and car payments that he has to look after. Their combined family income was just sufficient to cover the necessary expenses of a burgeoning family. He must have been given the impression that in my desperation, I was willing to give up all that kind of security.

To his consternation, I mentioned to him in no uncertain terms that the very reason that I was leaving was the same reason why he was staying—the S word. As a good friend, while I expected him to listen, I did not expect him to agree. I took the pains to explain to him in further detail.

Not to imply that my friend is a born pessimist; he expressed concerns about how I would meet my family obligations should my planned venture fail. Obviously, he is not the type who would take calculated risks. He would rather just wallow in the quagmire of indifference and wait for better opportunities to come by—with the proviso, however, that he would not put his guaranteed monthly check on the line. I could clearly see his point and, even clearer, the pity and commiseration written all over his face. To him, mine was a drastic move, unorthodox and absolutely audacious. They have debated about my departure around the watering hole, sometimes in hushed whispers, within their quiet circles from all possible angles. Most of them agreed on one thing—mine was not a smart move.

I left with a mixed bag of emotions. I was sad, because irrespective of what transpired in the workplace that has by now become unexciting to wake up to each morning, I made good friends, and we developed that kind of esprit de corps that easily transformed into maturity by constant association, mutual respect, and faith in the goodness of one another and human nature. I was happy, because after a painful mulling over of the possibilities elsewhere, I had no doubt in my mind that my gut feeling was right. My talent, time, and treasure could only be maximized in the business world where I belong.

I knew then as I know now that success comes by sticking to your plans. While I left not without trepidation, I also knew that I should not act on my fear. I told this to my friend because by that time, he felt that I was consumed in a cosmic cataclysm of some sort. I promised them that whatever happened in my chosen change of career, they would be the first to know. In the final analysis, I was gladdened to inform them that all the loose ends have been tied up and that I am managing quite successfully and enjoying my business.

That decision to leave my job was initially a disappointment for my friend. I am happy to tell them now that it is not one of the few regrets that I have in my life.

Security is to know that you earn the same amount of income regardless of the effort you put in. In order to justify its existence, the company union makes sure of that. Salary levels are based on position and seniority. Everybody is paid the same, regardless of ability and production capacity. With no offense intended to those concerned, there is a circulating joke in the public service sector that it takes an average of three years for one to reach his or her level of incompetence. This levity, of course, is taken fairly in jest.

If you are lucky, the only pay increases are the union-negotiated ones. It is very unfortunate that some people are so thoughtless that they resort to sarcasm like when some employees try to exert some extra effort, not really to impress but to show appreciation by doing what they are expected in exchange for their regular checks. It is not uncommon to hear remarks like, "Are you a stockholder of the government now?" If it is of any consolation, it is safe to say that stultifying remarks like this can only emanate from negative and miserable people of low breeding.

One disadvantage of employment is that the pay could be as steady as a rock but fixed like a flagpole. For an aggressive and ambitious person, this could be a confection for encouragement to look for a better, more challenging or a satisfactorily rewarding endeavor.

Our debts require monthly payments, and children need our unflinching financial support. A steady income can satisfy that, but it could be just right or sometimes inadequate.

Paying mortgages or massive credit card debts could take a lifetime to satisfy. With the limited income from employment, piecemeal payments can mean that by the time the house is paid and other liabilities are settled, there would be an empty nest. All the children will be independent. Business gives one a better leverage to a more comfortable lifestyle or retirement buffer starting at a much younger age.

Business Advantages

We learned in the previous chapter that we cannot simply conjure a preferable ending like they do in the movies or write a politically correct script for the audience to appreciate. The dilemma is that when we are employed, our employer has the upper hand, controlling our every move, while in business, the customers take the place of the demanding chief and are always right. Which one is preferable?

Between the demanding employer or a picky customer, which is preferable? You have more influence on your business affairs. It has been said that when you are in business, you still have to work eight hours but then you decide which time of the day is most suitable for you without compromising your business results. When you are employed, you need to show up for work at a designated time slot, and your priority is work.

The most important difference between employment and business is the control you have over your earning activities. The flexibility you have over issues such as managing time, budgeting finances, and assigning people make the latter challenging and the choice more appealing to responsible people.

There is more negotiation for profit's sake in business wherein the owner can leverage his or her position. It has been said that "you do not always get what you deserve; you get what you negotiate."

The government knows the importance of business. The burden of creating jobs is not only borne by the government but the business itself. Even small businesses are considered to be excellent generators of employment. The operators of businesses contribute the most to the economic progress of the country. For that reason, numerous tax advantages are available only to businesspeople.

There are allowable expenses that can be deducted from the income of businesses such as meals and travel expenses or representation allowances, which are the envy of the working class. For a more sufficient explanation, you could consult the professional services of an accountant.

In business, you can minimize or avoid paying tax but not evade through some legitimate means, depending on whether or not they are considered legal under the law. To some extent, there is flexibility on this as the regulations blur considerably as the government offers some leeway for the business to function in a viable manner. In the worst-case scenario, the claim can be rejected without further action. This is to be contrasted with tax evasion, which means one tries to avoid paying the required tax after due deliberation. This could result in fines, interests, prison terms, or all of the above.

Business Disadvantages

As an employee, under favorable circumstances, one can choose which nook or cranny one wants to be in as a favorite working spot and work happily as a clam. Accommodations due to physical or mental needs could be made available for better productivity and as mandated by law.

To go into business, one has to know how to handle potential enemies because they will come in droves and in waves—understandably, as the tendency is to have a piece of the action, to have a cut of the cake or profit.

Conflicts in business could be person against person, or person against nature or *force majeure*, referring to the slings and arrows of outrageous fortune. It could be you against another person, related by blood or not. When it comes to money, rivalry can be within your own family, which would be tragic. The biblical admonition says that a family fighting against itself will never thrive—brother against brother, father against son. Knowing how to handle this crisis could make or break any business deals and relationships. A good businessperson is always a lightning rod for criticisms and diatribes, and attracts enemies the way whales collect barnacles.

The toughest conflict to handle is that of a person against himself or herself. We can be our own worst enemies. It is important to reflect and know what we want in life and in the business that we decide to embark on. Somehow, we will regret some of our decisions and blame ourselves for them. But no matter what we do, that should not be a deterrent to move on. If we make mistakes, we have to accept them. It is not the number of times we fall, so the bard says, but the number of times that we rise after each fall. In the end, we will realize that even mistakes or crises are open opportunities. Then success will be its own reward.

Speaking of which, success could be one's own cause of countless aggravations and distractions. As honey would invariably attract flies, money from your business could attract an annoying number of solicitations for all kinds of worthy and dubitable charitable causes. Ironically, as a businessperson, you could be at the bottom of other people's social registers, but once your business success spreads like wildfire through the grapevine, you are on top of it in terms of donations. While there is nothing wrong with sharing your good fortune, it may be prudent to determine how much you are willing and able to offer for charity. Again, it begins at home, so it is wise to tend to all your obligations and needs first.

A story is told about an exceedingly affluent man who wanted to announce at his eightieth birthday party how he was going to divide his fortune in the event of his death.

In a low guttural voice, he said, "Ladies and gentlemen, I am happy to announce to you that half of my total assets will go to my children.

"The other half will go to charity. So please allow me to introduce to you my children and my wife, Charity."

People think you have a bottomless well full of cash where others come to make a bailout wish. At this point, you realize that at no time henceforth until your well runs dry will you ever be wanting of relatives. You will notice that even your enemies will follow the friendly path. They may come from all walks of life, be of all ages, and come from any place imaginable. Since there is nothing you can do about it because that is life, you might as well enjoy the virtue of giving. For after all, as in the sport of boxing, it is better to give than to receive.

Success is relative, the *Peanuts* cartoon said: the more success, the more relatives.

Blood is thicker than water, someone said. We need to understand, however, that just because one is close to you by virtue of a blood relationship does not necessarily mean that he or she would be a fellow selfless caretaker of your business with the same assiduousness as a good shepherd who takes care of his flock. This is the hard part, the dangerous fault line. There is a cautionary tale about the incremental steps that can lead your business into disaster.

With the best of intentions, you can decide to be helpful to your siblings or close relatives or close friends, almost to a fault. After all, charity begins at home. However, they could turn into either a mighty ally or a massive headache. It turns out that before you realize it, surreptitiously, they are bleeding you dry. While you may not want to jeopardize your relationships, this is one instance when you have to take a solid stance to stand by and save your business by reason of self-preservation.

Who?

If we build on our answer from the previous paragraphs, you just look for the person whose family tree has more branches than a weeping willow. There is your man.

In every profession, there are people who are best suited for particular jobs and responsibilities. The job interviews are designed to determine the most appropriate candidate and are conducted by experienced employees or business owners who learned and mastered the ropes. They also are experts in not letting the ropes hang them.

In business, however, there is no one to scrutinize your capabilities, character, and suitability. All one has to do is put pebbles in one's mouth and in the stentorian voice of Demosthenes shout to the world that from now on you are in business.

Some of these entrepreneurs succeed right away. The others have to keep being persistent. But first, they have to overcome the strenuous objections of unsolicited advisers, starting with their spouses if they are married. It is a Herculean job to say the least! For all and sundry to see, they might want to hang, in a conspicuous place, the bumper sticker that says, "Come in, buckle up, and shut up."

For some of the successful ones, their life stories are in the biography section of any bookstore; these tell their personal exploits, whether tragic or joyful! Television programs make movies about their adventures! We read them for inspiration, especially those rags to riches tales. It makes us think that God is merciful, and we are just a shower away.

Who qualifies as the best businessperson? The answer is as difficult as predicting next year's weather. You cannot pick the best candidate simply by scanning the crowd. The signs are not as visible as the morning sun on a clear day.

Keep in mind that the person with the best voice is not always the best singer! Some of the popular stage performers have raspy sounds like Rod Stewart or pronounced nasal resonance like Barbra Streisand. Burt Bacharach is a classic example!

Burt's singing voice does not have the best timbre, but he sings well and in tune. Best of all, he creates his own music with Hal David writing the lyrics. When Burt sings, nobody goes home. The queen of England enjoyed the command performance given in Burt's honor at the Royal Albert Hall.

He knows what the audience wants and makes sure they get their money's worth in every concert he gives. He always does his best performance. Even the high notes he loves to fill his compositions with, though seemingly uncomfortable, always sound pleasant. Burt does not need us "to say a little prayer for him." He knows his path around a successful music career, especially "the way to San Jose."

While businesspeople have individual differences like all of us, they have common characteristics that make them succeed. Let us take a look at a few sample traits from a list of plenty.

Ability to Make Decisions

The most obvious difference between a businessperson and the rest of the population is the ability to make unflinching decisions. To demonstrate this point, let us look at a case where two people of diametrically opposite views are arguing, and a third person is asked to decide whom he thinks is right.

If this appointed judge is a businessperson, the supporting views of the combatants would be heard and analyzed, and then a judgment would be rendered on the merits of each position.

On the other hand, if the judge is not a businessperson, both opponents would be declared winners. If a fourth person would express disapproval because of the opposite points of view, this judge would readily agree that he too is right.

Every day, we make decisions. There is no way we can avoid them. It could run the gamut of deciding what to do with a teenager who comes home one day with enough lip piercings that he or she resembles a zipper, which gives meaning to the expression "zip your lips up." It could be as easy as making up one's mind about the kind of appropriate apparel to wear for the day.

It is most difficult if the reluctant brain you are trying to convince is your very own. You do not have the benefit of telling it to mind its own business, to leave you alone, or to take a walk.

Why is this so important? All of us make daily decisions, simple, compound, and complex. As individuals, we do not always affect the lives of other people. In business, however, others are impacted by our actions and decisions, sometimes drastically.

Next time you go shopping, note the process by which women and men choose the items they want to buy. Call it biological differences, but the practice of buying clearly differentiates males from females.

Women love to try clothes even if the apparel is out of their price range and anatomical dimensions. Just trying on for size is the frequent justification. On one hand, females are not so concerned with the cost. Heaven forbid if anyone catches them wearing the same outfit twice or if another person is wearing the same attire.

Males, on the other hand, are proudest for clothes they own that have lasted them for centuries. The costs—or "damage," as men prefer to call expenses—make them reconsider going on another shopping excursion.

Making decisions requires commitment, something we do not give without the benefit of second thoughts. Sometimes, we need what the industry calls a cooling period. Therefore, many deals like real estate are required by law to honor retraction before a set date of firming up the contract.

As children, we rely on our parents to decide for us, until we reach the age of reason, sixteen to twenty years old, depending on where you live. That could be any age within the range, depending on where you are and what action you would like to do. Sometimes, the laws of the land are already made, and the government makes the decision for us, such as to attend elementary and high schools.

At work, employers require the employees to consult them before deciding anything critical and of value. You can be in hot water for taking that responsibility. The conventional wisdom is that failure is an orphan while success has plenty of parents.

The truth is that when making decisions, we simply lack practice. How can we not? We are occupied most of the time from making decisions.

Oftentimes, the primary reason it is difficult to decide is the insufficient knowledge we have on the subject matter or the nagging doubts we have about the effectiveness of our actions.

The ability to make decisions is the paramount qualification when you want to identify the businessperson. These are the people with opinions about everything and anything. You will not know it because they keep their impressions to themselves. They are lavish in their praises to others but stingy in offering advice about what to do. This is not because they are selfish by nature but because they understand that others have to make up their own minds too. More importantly, the ability to implement the suggestion depends on the executor. More importantly, they expect to be paid for their advices. Suggestions are dished out free of charge.

Opinions are easy to obtain because they are free, while advice is paid for, oftentimes at a very high price. The proverb that a lawyer's counsels are worthless unless paid for illustrates the point. A person who can decide knows the difference. That is not to say that mere suggestions are always discarded; after all, there are times when the best things in life are complimentary.

The main thing is that one cannot go into business if others are making decisions for you. Yes, a businessperson always consults; he or she has experts on retainers around to advise him or her about what to do, but in the end, the final act taken is his or her choice. He or she gathers data, digests it, and considers the ramifications, and then makes a conclusion. That is his or her primary responsibility.

Responsibility

In the business hierarchy, the best-qualified person to handle business is the individual who can accept responsibilities. It is coincidental maybe, but the word *responsibility* itself also implies the ability to respond to any given situation with the available resources.

Harry S. Truman left us with the immortal phrase "the buck stops here," connected with the expression "pass the buck," which means passing the responsibility on to others. The two-and-ahalf-by-thirteen-inch sign that was conspicuously displayed on his desk in the White House helps to explain why some people cannot become financially prosperous.

The word *buck* could be interpreted two ways. It could refer to responsibility or the US dollar. A buck is a sheep, which in the past was valued at a dollar. Passing the buck, referring to responsibility dodgers, is like living in the gutters of Easy Street, free of care and responsibility. Like the mendicant at the mercy of passersby, the person who passes the buck would rather live a life of begging for food rather than have the responsibility to enter a decent-paying job. He or she just waits for the blessing of the almighty buck.

It is the height of irresponsibility to be in a workplace and refuse to perform certain functions just because it is not in one's job description. While it may be true that one does not have to do the particular work, it is incumbent on us as employees for the good of the company and our fellow workers to do something outside the province of our designated work. That is true if the situation demands it. A case in point is when one has to stay a bit longer than the designated hour while waiting for a late fellow employee to arrive because he cannot just abandon his post.

To some extremists, the job description is the Magna Carta that one invokes when asked to do anything outside of what is required to justify his or her pay according to the provisions of the collective bargaining agreement. Union aficionados stick to the decreed requirements with hardly any elbowroom for justifiable deviations. Any action to the contrary is always referred to the grievance committee, which would understandably make legal counsels busy.

The line blurs between paid service and service that is done pro bono as the need arises. In the grand scheme, this extra service rendered or extra goods given will even out somehow. The reward or justified remuneration of such goodwill may not be immediate and obvious, because of its nature. In the end, it does not escape being considered valuable and appreciated. In the long run, the payback becomes twofold or even more as a natural consequence.

This brings us to the concepts of growing up and maturity. These point to the idea referring to the psychological and not the chronological age of an individual. This is a prerequisite for a person to be responsible. A twenty-year-old can act as if he or she is ten and vice versa. The former we consider childish or immature, while the latter is precocious or responsible. A person who acts his or her age is developing normally. That is the age of dependability. This is a valuable trait that prepares us for a higher economic level, a prelude to wealth accumulation. What is an economic level, and why is it important?

Economic Level

Why is it that a person's place in the economic hierarchy is important? It is because it defines your financial capabilities and determines your standing in business and society. It is the scorecard of wealth acquisition and maintenance, for success is not a one-shot deal accomplished with a single home run. It is a continuous game to the last inning. As Yogi Berra said, "It is not over 'til it's over," until the fat lady sings. Does that indicate to bloat financially?

In our struggle through life, we dream of financial independence, a relative term that can be interpreted millions of ways. Most of us have an average mortgage for an average house. Trump, on the other hand, has a mortgage, if any, for a mansion in Palm Beach, Florida. Trump's real estate taxes alone could pay the mortgage of several homes in the suburbs of Toronto. Add the ground and building maintenance, and you can have a vacation home in Cancun, Mexico.

For a fraction of Trump's monthly budget, we could see an end to our financial worries, retire, and enjoy the balance of our earthly existence traveling around the other parts of the world that we have yet to see and explore. It would be on a grand scale that would dwarf the voyages of Columbus and Magellan combined; we would have a suntan like George Hamilton on the Queen Elizabeth luxury ship.

Ironically, unlike so many people, those who are considered well off in life are the ones who would rather continue working, harder and longer. That makes us question their intentions or character quality—whether or not they enjoy wallowing in their greed with no satisfaction in sight until death do they part with their wealth. The answer of the Lord Thomson of Fleet is that, if that is the case, "he is not going."

Businesspeople seem to set their eyes on the high heavens and see an endless continuum of their quest for life. Unlike the common person, they enjoy the quest for fortune and get addicted to it, in a manner of speaking. Therefore, to satisfy their craving for selffulfillment, they hitch their wagons to a star. They own the firmament, and they bask in their glory. They sense a state of euphoria, a nirvana of some sort. They feel unhappy with anything less. On the other hand, the regular person stops short, far below the star hanging precariously.

"The day I do not enjoy what I do is when I stop," said Evel Knievel, who had broken 433 bones in his body with his motorcycle deathdefying stunts. He may be considered incorrigibly careless with unfettered bravado by some. Others admire him for being admirably careful, as he is quick to claim that he would rather be driven by Stevie Wonder than by one who is under the influence.

With an estimated net worth of approximately $60 million when he passed away in 2007 and with several unbroken Guinness world records, one would think that a dozen broken bones would have been enough to make him quit risking his life. He could become a quadriplegic or die. There are only 206 bones in the adult human anatomy. He had to fracture each bone twice with 21 more to break to have a count of 433. He must have been an orthopedic surgeon's worst nightmare as well as the most profitable purse string at the same time.

His orthopedic surgeon must have been good because Evel's death was not bone related. He succumbed to idiopathic pulmonary fibrosis. At his resting place in Butte, Montana, he must have a hearty chuckle every time he sees us hopelessly scared with some minor, inconsequential mishap or concerns similar to breaking only a pinky.

How much risk is considered reasonable? How much money can a person spend? If Warren Buffet were to give Cheryl Gillespie, the host of the TV program *Let's Shop*, her shopping allowance, she would need countless episodes and seasons to exhaust Warren's money even if she concentrated and purchased only the expensive items.

The irony is that Mr. Buffet does not believe in buying anything considered luxurious. Considering his excessive wealth, he lives rather an austere life worthy of a religious cleric. He lives in a three-bedroom old house that he owned for years in Omaha, Nebraska. At seventy-seven years old in 2008, he has joined financial forces with Bill and Melinda Gates for philanthropic charities.

That begs the question, After all these years of astronomically successful wealth acquisition, isn't it mind-boggling to think that Buffett and other philanthropists would give their fortunes away for free without batting an eyelash and with no return expectations? Did they not just waste their time doing business, earning huge chunks of wealth, only to hand it out to others? The only logical answer is to invoke what St. Francis of Assisi said in his prayer: it is in giving that we receive; it is in pardoning that we are pardoned; it is in dying that we are born to eternal life.

Buffett did not only enjoy the business of earning money. He also took pride and derived self-satisfaction using the same money to help others who were less fortunate. This is one instance when we can say that it is considerably easier for this rich man to enter the kingdom of heaven than for the biblical camel to enter the eye of the needle.

Buffett showed to the whole world that indeed happiness and greed do not peacefully coexist in the same sentence. The love or greed for money is the root of all evil. For his part, he made money as his means to an end and not the end itself. He earned money first the old-fashioned way and then used it, instead of him being used by his money, to help others in financial straits. He realized that death, the greatest equalizer, will separate him from his material wealth, so there is only one logical thing to do. What he does not use in this life, he shared with others with a big smile on his face. Deep in his heart, he knows that indeed, "It is not what we give but what we share, for the gift without the giver is bare." After all, everybody loves a cheerful giver. That is pure and simple philanthropy. It is charity, not Charity, the wife of the other wealthy man, in its most distilled form.

Among his legacies that he will leave the world is not only his wealth but also his priceless wisdom. Buffett keeps telling us, "Take some risk as I do." What he means, of course, is reasonable risk, not just any risk. Do we have the capability to take risks?

Capabilities of the Risk-Takers

An interesting story circulating in the motivation circuit is about the full-grown elephant in the circus being restrained by a small rope tied to a stake fastened to the ground. It is obvious that the pachyderm could simply snatch the restraining rope but does not.

The reason is simply psychological. At an early age, this animal was trained to obey the rules with the same size and strength of rope. But as a young elephant, it was not capable of wrenching the restraint.

As the elephant grew, its strength increased, but the experience of the past was fresh in its memories. These giants are supposed to have very long recollections. The presence of a rope tied to a leg automatically signaled to the beast's brain that it was not possible to break free. It had been conditioned to think that way. It would not even try.

Experiences at young ages have profound effects on the characteristics of a person. Phobias are good examples. Once fear is implanted in our brains, it takes time for counseling to rid us of its detrimental consequences.

Fortunately, positive mental attitude training has the same long-lasting effects. It is also interesting to note that the champions in any sports start usually at early ages. Like business ventures, sports require long bouts of performances before one reaches the pinnacle of success. If you start your vocation late, or you are a delayed bloomer, you know you have a lot of catching up to do. It is not impossible though, as you will see in the desire section on motivation in this book.

Tiger Woods began his interest in golf as a young boy under the protective wings and influence of his father, who so patiently developed his then-latent talent to play the game. Somehow in their minds, they both wanted to excel far beyond anybody's dream. They had to aim high to reach new heights.

Again, it was not easy, but they enjoyed the sport and did many practice rounds aspiring toward excellence, or close to perfection.

Jack Nicklaus, for instance, was asked once if he really considered himself lucky basking in the success of his profession as a champion golfer. He said he did but was quick to add, "And the more practice I do, the luckier I become."

His wife, when asked how she contributed to the success of her husband, said with a dash of jesting superstition, "Whenever he goes out to play for a major golf tournament, before he leaves our house, I pray for him and kiss his balls." Those were the balls Jack's personal caddy is not allowed to keep.

It is amazing what champions do to reach the pinnacle of glory, knowing that it matters to be number one because to be a mere second is to be the first loser. Lance Armstrong, the seven-time Tour de France champion, made this clear in a statement he made in an interview. Unfortunately, due to doping controversy, he got stripped of the titles.

These athletes became champions because they have the capabilities and believe they can win and want to win. They took the risks, and it paid off. If they had doubts, these athletes employed sport psychiatrists to turn around their faltering attitudes.

Athletes have to train their bodies to tolerate extreme pain. Business people have to accept unlimited amounts of risk. Like thespians on the stage, they mask their pain and miseries; you will not see it on their faces. They have what is called in Yiddish *chutzpah*.

Chutzpah: Only Qualification You Will Ever Need

Many businesspeople are ostracized for appearing uneducated and unsophisticated. A typical example was the late Henry Ford. A Detroit newspaper branded Henry as an "ignoramus." Ford sued the newspaper for libel.

During the ensuing trial, the lawyers of the defendants tried so hard to prove the ignorance of Henry Ford by asking him all kinds of questions from mathematics to geography. Alex Trebek could use these questions for several episodes of *Jeopardy*. Insulted, Henry replied, "Why would I bother myself with petty information when all I have to do is push a button and an employee of mine comes rushing with the answer?"

Henry Ford did not bother himself with general knowledge. He had specific technical expertise, which made him the undisputed authority on manufacturing automobiles. Henry Ford is the consummate engineer and designer of the combustion engine. He had 161 US patents under his name.

But most of all, like all successful people, Henry Ford had chutzpah, or guts. It is hard to succeed with courage alone, but without nerves of steel, no business sees the light of day. One wonders if Henry Ford's nerves of steel were stronger than the metals he used for his automobiles. One thing you can be sure of is that the thousands of people under his employ must have worshipped the very ground that he walked on and genuflected in front of his picture displayed in the factory floor. He was their undisputed patriarch and leader of unflinching ability.

Leadership

If you are not a born leader, the best place to learn leadership is to get yourself accepted at a reputable military school. These schools will make a leader out of you, whether you like it or not. The problem is that these schools, such as the US Military, Naval, and Air Force Academies, have very strict admission requirements, especially with age. The minimum age for the US Air Force Academy is seventeen, and the maximum is twentythree. Outside of this age range, you are out of luck.

The issue of leadership has the same predicaments with salesmanship (see chapter 5). Are leaders born or made? It really doesn't matter whether the ability is congenital or learned; you have to know how to lead.

When you decide to go into business, usually it is because you are infected with the leadership bug. You want to be president of your own company or country, but you do not have your own personal real estate or country.

There are many kinds of leaders: military leaders like Alexander the Great, Napoleon Bonaparte, General Patton, and so on; heads of state; company presidents; and leaders of different organizations.

Some are authoritarian leaders; others are liberals, Democrats, and Republicans. In a nutshell, the authoritarian leader says, "I know where you want to go, so I will lead you there." On the other hand, the democratic leader says, "Tell me where you want to go, and I will lead you there." What style is best for you? Only you can decide.

J. Paul Getty stated in his book *Life as I See It, Life as I Lived It* that he liked to hire people who were experts on the subject of humanity. They are genuinely interested in and understand people very well; therefore they could lead them. The best vitamin for leadership is B1; experts say they are also expert communicators.

Ability to Communicate

The ability to communicate clearly and effectively is critical when you are in business because there are many people around you who must be informed precisely of your intentions and requirements. Misunderstanding can be very costly and time-consuming.

Failure to communicate is probably the number one reason for relationship breakdown. Legal counselors can attest to the validity of this statement. Hearing is not always listening. The same is true with merely talking. Speaking is not always communicating.

There are three parts of communication: the sender, the receiver, and the message. Failure to communicate could happen during the transmission from the sender to the recipient or within the message itself.

Here is an example of a typical communication in any household.

Spouse 1: Honey, can you get my car keys? They are in the bedroom.
Spouse 2: I cannot find them. Where did you put them?

Spouse 1: They are in the top drawer of the cabinet on the right side of the bed. Are you blind or something!
Spouse 2: Yes, I am, so you get them yourself!

Spouse 1 is fully aware of the whereabouts of the item in question; therefore, to communicate the precise information to spouse 2 seems unnecessary. Do not get upset when there is a failure of understanding and delivery. This is typical. All the ill feelings would have been avoided had the message been crystal clear. Compounding the aggravation is the uncalled-for remark. Remember "a sharp tongue may cut your throat," according to Chinese wisdom.

Teachers and professors are the worst offenders of the theories of communications. The mandate of the teacher is to ramble on the subject matter just to complete his job regardless how much the students assimilate. Failure in class is always the fault of the student not the incompetent teacher whose pedagogical acumen is kept in the bank deposit vault.

The late former US president Ronald Reagan was known as "the great communicator." The ability to communicate can be learned and mastered, according to George Merlis, the former producer of *Good Morning America*. Reagan demonstrated this ability when he got shot by John Hinckley on March 30, 1981. He humorously told his wife, Nancy, "Honey, I forgot to duck."

Who could forget the answer he gave during the presidential debate of 1984? He quipped, "I am not going to make age an issue of this campaign. I am not going to exploit, for political gains, my opponent's youth and inexperience." We all wish to have the ability to inject humor in tight situations.

If you have all these qualifications, such as leadership, the ability to make decisions, responsibility, and excellent communication skills, when is the right time to throw your betting hat into the ring?

When?

The classic business story about when one should go into business is about Colonel Harland Sanders of KFC when we are referring to age. The colonel started his fowl-frying business when most people retire: at a ripe old age of sixty-five. The military rank of Colonel Sanders was for promotional purposes, but it is important to note that he had been perfecting his cooking techniques long before that.

Unlike political positions, there is nothing in the Constitution that states when anyone can involve himself or herself in business. There is no plan to introduce any legislation to limit the entry of anybody. It is not covered by a child labor law. Like the boy pharaoh who became king at an early age, you can crown yourself a businessperson as soon as you can operate a cash register.

The moment you have learned the four items in the "Who" section, you are almost complete and prepared. The most appropriate answer, then, is anytime: whenever you are ready to get set and then go.

The Age Factor

T. Boone Pickens said in an interview that he started business at an early age with a paper route. Warren Buffet claimed to have started at age fourteen. That was several billion dollars ago.

The moment you have infected yourself with the entrepreneurial bug and have acquired and mastered the qualifications to operate a business, take off your Fedora like Oddjob, the henchman of *Goldfinger*, and throw your hat in the entrepreneurial ring not at the neck of a concrete statue.

The last quarter of the twenty-first century produced several billionaires under the age of forty. It is true when they say the earlier the better. Besides, it will give you more time to enjoy the fruits of your labor, feast with the epicurean chefs of Le Cordon Bleu in Paris, drink Dom Perignon in the Riviera, try to break the hustlers of Las Vegas, and, better still, have your own private island in Hawaii or the Caribbean.

Age is supposed to be just a state of the mind. Wolfgang Amadeus Mozart did his first composition at age five. He had composed more than six hundred pieces at the time of his death at age thirty-five. Mozart probably wrote his first piano concerto piece on the living room wall in their house in Salzburg with a crayon, to the dismay of his parents.

The commanding sound of our parents still reverberates when we want to know the answer to the next question: When should I start? The answer is *now* in spite of your health.

The Health Factor

Stevie Wonder was asked the question, "What is the hardest thing about being blind?" He responded without hesitation: "You can't see," to the laughter of the audience.

The interviewer expressed and feigned sympathy. Stevie commented in a smart quip, "Do not pity me; sympathize with the people who can see but have no vision." Witty retort maybe, but it has plenty of wisdom in it. Stevie did not wait for medical technology to make him see; it did not bother him; he saw no reason for it. Why should he? He does not need to close his eyes to visualize a million bucks brightly shining within grasp.

Andrea Bocelli makes more money than many of us. A man like him may not have the gift of sight, but he has foresight; he's endowed with a positive attitude and $1 million worth of vocal cords. Andrea is a singer extraordinaire, producer, songwriter, and a virtuoso musician. In addition, he can expertly play the keyboard, saxophone, flute, harp, trumpet, trombone, guitar, and drums. Every part of his anatomy is beating in harmony with the music, to the envy of a frustrated music maker. Whether he is beating his own drums, blowing his own horn, or strumming his own guitar, he is proclaiming to the world, "Hey, listen, there is music in me."

There is a story about a man who was complaining because he had no shoes until he saw people without feet. You no longer have to wait until you can grow a foot. You can now be fitted with prosthetic legs.

Countless people with disabilities have accomplished great deeds considering their disabilities. Stephen Hawking is the undisputed dean. He was afflicted with amyotrophic lateral sclerosis. He was known for his theories on black holes, theoretical cosmology, and quantum gravity. That proves once again that limits are human made not due to maladies. This frail and seemingly incapable man, with his capabilities and mental faculties though severely restricted, contributed still to make this world a better place.

Tony Melendez, a Latino and a man who can play his string instrument with just his feet, is more proficient than a man with both hands. He was not dissuaded by his congenitally absent arms but gets his kicks strumming his *la guitarra* with his right foot while belting out the lyrics of his tune. Is it because his Latino race got him rhythm?

The Race Factor

The conventional belief was that race is permanent until Michael Jackson proved them wrong. Anyone can alter the epidermal pigmentation after all. The world has changed with the times, and for the first time, an African American president was elected. Barack Obama did not even have to change his hair to the color purple. He just made sure Oprah Winfrey was on his side.

The fact is that race is no longer an impediment to success. The only hindrances now are a negative mental attitude and a failure to understand the hows of business. There should be no barrier to educating yourself with productive knowledge. So what is there to stop you? Repeated pleading or complaining like a broken record will lead you nowhere.

Rhythm and Flamboyance Factor

The aptitudes that require a Herculean effort to acquire are the perfect rhythm or timing and flamboyance, because these are congenital traits that are cultivated through your formative years. One could train for years to be a public speaker, but if the butterflies in your stomach keep flying at random instead of in formation, you will not be able to think effectively standing up, let alone speak legibly and cogently.

It is like a neophyte comedian relating the same jokes of a veteran comic, wondering why none of the audience crack even a smile while the latter makes the listeners roll in the aisle with laughter.

President Donald Trump is a classic example of a practitioner of the art of perfect rhythm and flamboyance in his negotiating strategies. The ballet dancer Mikhail Baryshnikov's timing to the beat is impeccable and with such graceful execution that he leaves the audience breathless in enjoyment.

Flamboyance, on the other hand, is your demeanor in relation to others. Gestures, they say, are the outward expression of your inward intentions. It is interesting to note that pantomime is a subject thoroughly studied by students of method acting. Norma Desmond of *Sunset Boulevard* fame claimed she could tell a whole story simply by telegraphing messages through her eyes, all without uttering a word.

The caveat to the popular statement "If he/she can do it, so can I" is that the act is not difficult to follow, but the rhythm is a tough thing to emulate. Coupled with flamboyance needed, it is impossible to be somebody else. The trick is to be original; there is only one Elvis Presley or Peter Thiel, one of the founders of Paypal. Be a pioneer, a trendsetter if you can. Not so many fans admire a wannabe. There is only one you; discover your forte, develop it, and be the best you can be, short of joining the army.

The 3H Club of Business

How to Start a Business

The best way to start a business that will flourish as soon as possible is to go into the blooming business. You derive much pleasure seeing these buds develop until they wilt or somebody nips them in the stem. The thorny issue of marketing these blossoms is negated by the joys it will give, especially to the recipient of the fragrant gesture. If it is true that we can say our sentiments with flowers, learn the process to convince the taciturn to buy more than one stem and for once add to his words and expressions of love.

Starting a business is difficult at best, like turning on the car engine on a very cold winter morning with a weak battery. The motor oil viscosity is like molasses, and the starter crank sounds like a seal gasping for air.

Your favorite car gives you the cold shoulder, and there is no one there to give you a boost. Even when the engine finally comes alive, you are still unsure of the conditions of the road. Will there be black ice or snow deeper than your tires? What do you do? If you are like most of us, you go back to bed and hope for better weather the next day.

The First Step

Most people in their adult years will encounter others who are seemingly content, seizing the fun of the day and without wrinkle in their faces, when asked what they do for a living. If the answer is that they are engaged in some kind of a venture, that explains their lavish lifestyle because they are just taking all wealth to the detriment of others. We remember the great business idea we incubated eons ago. We conclude it is time to revisit and catch up the lost revenue of years gone by.

Sage advice is not to bite off more than you could swallow. Many people mention capital as the number one reason not to go into business. Is it because they want to enter the business arena in a big way?

A paper route is appropriate when you are young because you can do it as a child. It is embarrassing to compete with children who are trying to earn some money for swimming lessons when you are old enough to drive them in their designated route.

You can do what T. Boone Pickens did as child. He started a newspaper distribution business, and then he took over the whole neighborhood. He tried to do the same thing as an adult in the oil and gas industry. Mesa Petroleum is a formidable player, and he is a billionaire. How is that for an ending? Mr. Pickens's life story cannot be covered in one book, let alone one paragraph.

Children of businesspeople are blessed due to the influences of their parents. The same is true with the children of artists, actors, and actresses. Michael Douglas got the acting virus at an early age from his parents for sure. The advantage is that their minds do not need convincing. These children believe it is the natural thing to do.

Unbeknownst to these children, they took their first sanguineous business step from birth. An investor father taught his daughter, who later on became a financial expert, to read by browsing the stock price listings in the newspaper. She learned the ABCs and high finance at the same time. One wonders if the company stock initials are more interesting than the highs and lows of the Dow Jones averages.

These protégés are surrounded by experts like their parents and their friends that they can learn from. For us who are not so fortunate to have first developed the thirst then, look for similar business surroundings. This means to acquire a strong and persistent desire and then learn all the things we need to succeed from books, through experimentations, or from research. When you happen to be in touch with successful businesspeople, pick their brains not their pockets.

When you are ready to test the business waters, decide what is a profitable business. If you are out of ideas, you may have to invent one.

The Invention Theory

If you have the Thomas Edison touch, try to invent something that will excite the buying public like the simple Hula-Hoop or an electrical gizmo that will revolutionize the modern home or office. It does not have to be technically complicated like magnetic resonance imaging (MRI). Giant companies like 3M make millions of dollars selling Post-it Notes. (These are multicolored, variable small rectangular pieces of paper with glue on the top edge.)

Whatever your bright idea is, you have to make a marketable sample—meaning complete with packaging and a UPC. You have to be ready to guarantee to the prospective buyers that you can deliver any volume of orders in the event they agree to purchase your product. This is one of the catch-22 situations of business.

Would you invest your life savings on an unproven product? What would happen if nobody buys your beloved gizmo? To manufacture a prototype is expensive, especially if you need complicated molds, even if you contract out the job to a low-cost country. There are many promotional expenses in taking your product into the marketplace. Once these costs are presented, including the patent cost, the business dream usually floats like a log in the raging rapids.

A more formidable problem of this approach for the neophyte businessperson is that he or she has not experienced the difficulty of establishing a distribution market for his or her goods or services. Should you establish the distribution system first? The marketplace is not a benign environment that is kind to anyone, beginner or veteran. If you think you have experienced a variety of disappointments, wait 'til you get lost in this marketing jungle. But without a product, how could you begin to tread the deep and murky swamps of marketing?

One solution is to establish a distribution system for imported products. You have a live sample, market friendly and ready. The manufacturing of these goods is the only concern of the importer. These goods come to you in a market-ready quantity. All you have to do is to bring it to your country of operation; therefore, you have to learn customs rules and regulations.

What are FOB (free on board), import duties, commercial invoices, bills of lading, letters of credit, and so on? FOB is a contradiction in terms because there is nothing free in the importation of goods except the samples you may have received. Take a course or at least buy a book on the subject if you want to learn the nitty-gritty details.

The Importation Theory

We dream of hitting the jackpot with an exotic product that we have the exclusive rights to distribute and sell like the proverbial hotcake. We may bump into these products during our travels, or a friend might have bought one somewhere but does not recognize the marketing potential.

Let's say you spotted an interesting gadget on a trip to Taiwan. You found the manufacturer and discovered that the item is not exported to your country, and they are willing to give you an exclusive right for a limited time while you are establishing the market.

You bought commercial samples and calculated the cost FOB to your base of operation. You come up with a selling price that is within range of what people would buy impulsively—say $30.00 retail.

We work backward for simplicity. If the target retail price is $30.00, the store would normally buy at a 50 percent discount ($15.00). If you have to go through a wholesaler, expect to dish out another 50 percent to your selling price. Now you are down to $7.50. This price should take into consideration all your importation costs, distribution, warehousing, and profit.

As you can see, when you solve one problem, another pops up. Your biggest headache is where to store your goods. If you have a spare garage, and your neighbors do not object, you can store your products there while you are growing your importation business. Remember rental cost is a fixed expense that could gnaw your profits away in a hurry. Your speed in establishing your distribution system is the key component of this enterprise.

Businesses that deal with products have inherent problems, as you have seen in the previous paragraphs. Are you trying to consume a five-year supply of vitamins from a failed venture before the expiration date? So you finally have had it with products. Service does not need space except for your equipment.

The Service Business Theory

If inventory keeping is not your idea of an ideal business, providing services definitely will fit the bill. The equipment you will need can be rented as needed, thereby lessening the capital requirements. There are numerous problems associated with inventories, such as theft, spoilage, outdating, and the like.

A manpower agency is an excellent business providing staffing needs to companies, institutions, and the government. The agency provides all sorts of skilled workers such as accountants, secretaries, factory workers, temporary laborers, hospital staff like nurses and hospital attendants, and data processing personnel. Since you are dealing with human resources, it is best to practice the science of people relations by mastering the recommendations of Dale Carnegie in his book *How to Win Friends and Influence People*.

Service agencies cover personnel that are absent for a day, on leave, or sick. They also provide extra help during high seasons of the hospitality industry or skilled workers during temporary increases in workload in places such as hospitals.

An enterprising person founded a maid service while another established a painting business using college students. Many services are needed to make our economy grow and thrive.

If you are attending school, one of the best places to start implementing your business ideas is in the institution you are attending.

The College Project Theory

The Google boys developed their business ideas at Stanford University. Their story is one for the business history books. It is difficult to think of Sergey Brin and Larry Page without feeling a touch of envy. Most of us will settle just to be a distant cousin of theirs.

Who can predict what the next Google opportunity will be? We can only be sure that somebody is already busy working out the business operational details. Who knows if in one of the classrooms of higher learning, an ambitious person is incubating an entrepreneurial dream that will perfect the artificial intelligence application.

We have seen people who have become billionaires who started their businesses at university, such as Michael Dell of Dell computers, Jeff Bezos of Amazon, and Mike Lazaridis of Research in Motion, and so forth. There is one undeniable fact about these people: they know what they want and are very knowledgeable about their crafts. In addition, they saw ways to apply their skills into business models that everybody else ignored and gained profits.

The Knowledge Factor Theory

All businesspeople must know something about the businesses they are in. For example, if you want to be in the garment business, you have to know the different types of fabrics, such as cotton, silk, wool, and the like. You should be able to evaluate quality like thread counts and weights.

You should have an understanding of the different machineries, but you do not have to be a skilled sewing machine operator unless you are also doubling as a worker. You do not have to be an expert fashion designer or haberdasher to have a taste for haute couture.

William Gates must be an expert in programming. He started by doing that. It is safe to bet that he could tangle with the best of the best, the top guns of the desktop operating system during his heyday. He could program the most byzantine routines and organize convoluted modules.

Bill could manage the elaborate steps for all the input/output devices to follow in order to communicate with the central processing unit, even when he was half-asleep.

His programming acumen is doubled by having a partner who is probably as good if not better than the guru himself. His name is Paul Allen. Between the two of them, they could make experts in the field look like amateurs.

After that, they started to clone themselves by hiring the cream of the computer programmer crop. Bill and Paul had their glory days, until another pair circled their personal computer wagon and gave a stiff headache that only a potent analgesic could alleviate.

They are the Google boys, who want to make obsolete the operating system developed by Bill, Paul, and company. It pays to know all the facets of your business, at least at the beginning. After that, you can start hiring employees who can improve on what you started. All you have to do now is manage.

How to Manage a Business

To the uninitiated, business management is just barking orders to subordinates, attending meetings, enjoying long lunches, and spending the profits. On the other hand, some people do not want to be in business because businesspeople have nothing but problems and heartaches. Nothing could be further from the truth than believing that business management is easy.

As we indicated several times in this book, only few would welcome the responsibility of managing a business. The reason is simple. It is difficult. It could drive you to the nut house or to the poor house if you are not careful.

No Experience Required

The first requirement for new recruits for a military institution is to have a burning desire to serve and to undergo rigorous training. Physical and mental abilities are honed to the armed services' standards.

Their bodies are whipped into shape to withstand the physical demands of the military. The dormant muscles are awakened to endure the new workload. Their minds are convinced to accept all forms of discomfort. It is like opening the pituitary nerve tap to allow endorphins to flow to suppress all sensations of pain.

All business neophytes should undergo the same initiation and be baptized by flaming desire. That way, they are ready to fight and their lymphocytes are activated to ward off any malady to infect their business plans. Managing a business is calling on all your reserved artillery of knowledge and acquiring new armaments such as the importance of understanding financial statements. In the chapter on financing, you will see where it is used and applied.

Any Tom, Dick, and Harry can form a golf resort corporation, call it Bogey, Eagle, and Birdie Inc. (BEB), and expect a hole in one performance even when their business abilities are way below par. Regardless of their entrepreneurial handicaps, no sand traps or ponds can dampen their eagerness to drive their enterprise ball into the driving ranges. They are determined to change traditions, believing they have a big Bertha club to do it.

Most people will admit that lack of capital is the number one reason for not engaging in business, but they will not admit they lack business knowledge. Just because Tom, Dick, and Harry are polished golfers, their expertise in the game does not guarantee an ability to run and manage a golf resort.

Even successful businesses have their Waterloo or, in keeping with the parlance, Augusta. In 2008, the three biggest automobile makers of America were flirting with bankruptcy. Their financial plights will be the case studies of MBA students for years to come.

How could behemoths like General Motors, Ford, and Chrysler, with their battalions of business experts, consultants, and establishment geniuses, misfire on all cylinders?

If these corps of outstanding abilities fail to foresee the incoming gloom, what are the chances for smaller companies to succeed? Did they become unmanageable because of their size? Conglomerate is best, but there are potholes and sand traps.

What they have is a one-ton gorilla. First, the left hand does not know what the right hand is doing. Those corporations are so big that only the Almighty knows what is going on. If that is not enough, the union said that they are not going to agree on concessions.

These companies are on life support and the auto workers union would not lessen its oxygen demands. The horseless carriage will need the stallion soon. If not, we are sure there are professionals itching to help.

The Professional Help

The moment we feel ready to break the champagne bottle and launch our venture ship, our first trip is a visit to the office of some professionals. With their expert guidance, we will avoid costly mistakes or at least hope to do so. The trio of the must-have professionals are skilled people in the know who could assist you to avoid problems before they occur or to assist you in times of trouble.

The Lawyer

If you are a fool, the proverb says, then you can be your own lawyer. But we are not hoodwinks, so we consult a lawyer for legal issues such as business registrations and setups. This expense is even more important in cases of partnerships. These barristers can make sure that the fine print will protect your interests, and in the event of dissolutions, you will not be left with unnecessary bills and liabilities.

Paying for legal invoices, especially at the beginning when finances are tight, seems unnecessary and expensive. You can choose to compensate the lawyers at the time of formation or at dissolution. The choice is yours.

During the operation of your business, you will be engaged in negotiations, making agreements with suppliers, investors, creditors, and so forth. It is best to find a lawyer you can rely on to protect your interests from the beginning.

It is true that some contracts are not worth the paper they are written on, but a written contract duly signed and witnessed makes the job of enforcement easier for professionals such as judges, police officers, and lawyers.

Ironclad contracts have been broken, and yours will not be the first or the last. It is very important to consider that litigation to be worth your time is if there is a loss of money. If this can be proven, by law, you should be compensated. If there is no financial damage or loss, you just fattened the purse of the lawyer.

Then you have the problem of collections. Can the defendant pay the award? Could you even find him or her afterward? If not, the only winners are the lawyers. You have to pay them, win or lose. What is the best legal advice?

Agree with the terms only when you can afford to waste the investment, should there be discord with the other party. If problems happen, walk away and then charge your losses to experience; it is better for the nerves and sanity.

To take account of your legal winnings and losses, you need an accountant, hopefully another excellent professional, on your side. Besides, he is the guy to count your beans and look after the taxation needs, for we have our silent but avaricious partner, the government.

The Accountant

Your business has not even begun to operate. What do we need an accountant for? Accountants are supposed to count the beans of our labor. The business seed has just been planted and registered; it has not yet germinated, let alone had fruits to count.

That is absolutely right if you do not need financing. The banker, as you will see in the next section, likes to see forms prepared by an accountant, preferably the certified kind.

If your parents are in business, they already have an accountant who knows you because he has included you as a dependent or an employee of your parents' company. In operating your business, your accountant's phone number should be on speed dial because there will be many instances when you would rather have him or her answer probing questions from authorities who have legal interests in your operation.

The revenue division is the paramount branch of the government. After them, you have to deal with labor, health, municipal, and federal, state, or provincial offices and a host of others. At the very least, you have to meet with your accountant twice a year to file your annual company income tax and personal returns.

Having an excellent accountant is like having a guardian angel for your business. He or she not only helps in accounting your finances but also advises you on important matters such as tax and estate planning. The best ones also know how to open a private numbered bank account in the Bahamas, Cayman Islands, Switzerland, Liechtenstein, Monaco, and so forth.

Like all professionals, accountants charge expensively for their services. That is because they know they play an integral part in your business operations. The only one who does not charge a direct fee is the friendly banker.

The Banker

To go into a business is to deal with the most vicious creature of all, the humanoid ilk of the great white shark and cousin to the crocodile. First, we dealt with the unconscionable lawyer, then the unscrupulous moneylender whose office is armed with the sharp sword of Damocles—speak about being in double jeopardy!

The malevolent reputation, justified or not, is alleviated by the fact that the banker is the only one who can open the bank vault for you. He or she decides whether you could avail yourself of the use of other people's money (OPM), a vital component in the principle of leveraging.

Leveraging is the process by which modest David could level the playing field with bulkier Goliath. The banker is the benevolent godfather you never had who provides you with the ability to finance a project beyond your available capital for larger returns on investments. Since the total profit is to divide the total net profit over the initial investment, it is possible that because of the increased capital due to the borrowed money, the profit ballooned, thereby resulting in a heftier return.

As long as the business operations can pay for the borrowing cost, meaning that the profit percentage is larger than the cost of borrowing, leveraging is an excellent method for increasing your participation in the market. Your friendly banker can provide you with the mechanism to accomplish that maneuver.

Before you can successfully engage the services of the bank, you will need to submit documents that show the viability of your plans and abilities as profit generator. The section on financing will explain this in detail. This is where you will need the help of your accountant.

If financing is needed, bankers would prefer that the forms are prepared by an accountant even if you could prepare your own documents. The accountant is a third party whose recommendations add more weight to loan requests. Besides, it is probably a bank policy to require one. Your credit application will be more credible, and you will look more experienced and professional.

It is best to establish a healthy business relationship with a lawyer, an accountant, and a banker long before your business commences. They are important friends to have even just for personal reasons.

With a talented entourage like them, you will be well armed and ready to rumble.

How to Maintain

Recruit, Train, and Retain

Employees are the lifeblood of any business. No business can survive without an adequate number of reliable employees. They make or break a business.

Managing people is the primary responsibility of a businessperson. The holy trinity of managing people is to recruit, train, and retain them. When Google started to tangle with the dominant arachnids of the internet, Microsoft knew they had an epidemic in their trap. Google venom prowled the internet web enticing the bright minds of the software companies to transfer to the up-and-coming star of technology.

A *Business Week* headline read, "Trouble Exits at Microsoft." Lee, a prized employee, had bolted to Google. The threat of a key employee exodus lurked in the background, a potential nightmare for the ubiquitous company.

There is no effective law to prevent a person from resigning and then working for a competitor. Yes, there are ramifications should the terms of employment be violated, but beyond compensation for money losses, the transfer of an employee is but a done deal.

Successful companies spend an enormous amount of money honing their recruitment programs. All internet sites have a section for employment opportunities. Headhunters, a manpower recruiting parlance, charge expensively for their services.

After an employee is hired, the expense of training this new recruit begins. There is a huge investment for educating new personnel. The knowledge these workers learn is important to help make your company profitable.

Contrary to popular belief, it is more difficult to hear the words "I resign" than to say, "You're fired." In both cases, you will have to hire a replacement, but the latter has become a liability. The employer has to decide. Dismissal is more welcome than working together in disharmony.

President Donald Trump popularized the phrase "You're fired." For his efforts, Trump wanted to own a trademark on the sentence. Apparently, he was denied. To maintain employees is a difficult balancing act. The technique is as varied as the number of employees you have because of individual differences. Understanding work culture is advantageous. North Americans react differently from Asians or Africans in different situations. The same statement can be construed as an insult in one race while it is a compliment in another.

The statement "You are losing weight" is welcomed by North Americans because it implies a healthy behavior, while it would indicate poverty to some cultures, thus having the opposite effect.

Telling a North American, especially a woman, that he or she is gaining weight is insulting, while in other cultures, this indicates prosperity. Practice political correctness. It is safer and is humorous at the same time.

Paul Getty is correct. An excellent understanding of humanity is an important quality to have when running a business along with emotional quotient. If you have an excellent relationship with your employees, it is easy to know who you can trust and rely on, an important part of delegating responsibility and authority.

To Delegate or Not to Delegate

As a business owner, your most important assets are your people. Therefore, it is important to master the art of delegating power and responsibilities.

As a leader, which you are, you delegate, which means you are free to do other important things. The art of delegating is to complete the process of duplication—the main advantage of entrepreneurship.

Employees or those who are selfemployed cannot avail themselves of this privilege. As an employee, you cannot negotiate a salary and then turn around and look for someone who is willing to render the service on your behalf at a lower price.

Even if you can do that, it won't be long before this rosy arrangement is terminated because your personal employee has been hired to replace you. For the self-employed, this is impossible because in most cases you probably have a license to practice that is nontransferable, such as legal and medical licenses.

The MustKnow Financial Statements

The most important financial statements the business owner must understand are the balance sheet and income expense statement. This book is not about bookkeeping, let alone accounting, but the business owner must have a good understanding of these documents to properly evaluate the performance of his or her business activities.

If Money Could Talk

The first step in an audit process is to scrutinize the financial statements starting with the bank record. The money trail, both deposits and withdrawals, will tell the whole story and tell how they were allocated. Following the money trail is the gospel truth in the auditing process.

The financial statements are the summary of the business activities, past and present. The balance sheet shows the business assets, liabilities, and owner equities. From here, one can determine the solubility of the business.

The last recession caused many companies to be insolvent, meaning they were running out of cash, and credit facilities had dried up like water in the Sahara in summer. From this statement, analysts can derive different ratios they can use for evaluations and make recommendations to creditors, investors, and owners. The health of the business can easily be determined from this report.

The income/expense statement, on the other hand, shows the cash flow activities of the business. Using the body analogy, if food is supplied in abundance and in excess of our calorie-burning rate, we store up energy. Unfortunately for the human body, this is stored as fat, which increases the size of our midsections or bottoms.

If our food consumption is like our business operation, we would have more income to offset our expenses. The difference is called profit. This is referred to as a healthy bottom line.

Should we operate our businesses the same way we dine, there would be no more bankruptcies and health problems. We would all live happily ever after.

The business owner must at the very least know how to read a financial statement. He or she does not need to know how to prepare one unless he or she is doing his or her own bookkeeping and tax preparations.

Financial statements are not only for business owners but for the revenue department of the government of your country. Words of caution: once signed, sealed, and delivered, this a legal document subject to the usual scrutiny and punishment, if there are discrepancies. It is for the bank for credit purposes and for potential investors and buyers of companies. The filed financial statement is construed as the truth even if you claim that there are camouflaged undeclared incomes. The value then will be assessed and will be declared accordingly.

Keep in mind that third parties who have interest in your business are interested to see only the copy of your tax forms filed with the revenue department.

The financial statements included in the revenue submissions are construed as the most genuine.

If Money Could Talk

For every benefit comes responsibility; as we have seen in the theories of business, there are advantages counterbalanced by disadvantages. To be a businessperson is to have or acquire skills and characteristics that could be uncomfortable for us, yet these must be adopted if we want to succeed.

To involve yourself in business is to develop characteristics that distinguish you from the rest of society. To succeed in business, you must act in a manner that even your closest friends and relatives could not understand. The saying "business is business" becomes your guiding principle, which could be strange to the people around you.

The most important thing to remember is that the seed of success must be sowed first in an environment that is conducive to a healthy and productive growth.

CHAPTER 3

Business Development

The Personalities of Businesses

From the government's viewpoint, there is not much distinction between people and businesses, especially in the area of taxation and liabilities. Business or an individual, both have unique personalities, yet from the eyes of the revenue department, these are one and the same. Simply put, Uncle Sam of the United States wants you to pay taxes regardless of your appearance. If the offender is a corporation, the law goes after the owners. The bureaucracy is the windmill of the quixotic world that sometimes makes this undertaking like an impossible dream.

Unlike the gender classifications, which is too numerous to count, there are only two or three business personalities, if you include the hybrid of the first. Here are just very brief discussions. Consult your lawyer and accountant for their recommendations.

Sole Proprietorship

Proprietorship oftentimes is the preferable option among the three, especially in the outset of the operation, not only because it is the simplest but because it is the easiest to wind down and dissolve if the plans are abandoned for some reason.

In Canada, Ontario in particular, to compose your entrepreneurial rhapsody is a simple trip to the Office of Consumer Affairs, where you must register your one-of-a-kind business epithet (name search required), pay the required fee, and then leave the commercial office jogging in rhythmic happy beat like a jolly sweet sixteen.

Before the registrar allows you to leave his provincial tollbooth, this officer must have given you a form to apply for a tax remittance number in anticipation of a hefty slice of your current income. You just acquired a silent associate to your venture, who will not shed even a drop of sweat in return for the cut you must reluctantly remit periodically.

The business activities are conducted in your name for the business. The distinct name is for segregating the income or loss of the business but directly attributable to your name, SS, or social security number in the USA, and SIN, social insurance number, in Canada.

Should there be more than one person registering the business, all parties must have a partnership agreement to officially launch the venture. In this scenario, you will have to go to the next paragraph.

Partnership

A partnership is a setup where parties, also called partners, agree to cooperate to advance their common business concerns. The partners in a partnership could be individuals, businesses, interest-based organizations, schools, governments, or combinations. Organizations may agree to increase the likelihood of each partner in achieving their goals and to increase their reach. In a partnership, for the protection of all parties involved, it is advisable to issue and form a holder of all equity that may be only controlled by a legally notarized contract.

It is very important to note that even the best of friendships can be wrecked by one dissenting opinion or a member being influenced by others. It is therefore advisable to protect yourself in the event of a nonamicable dissolution so that you won't suffer a tremendous financial loss.

Corporation

There is nothing more flamboyant than to proclaim that we are the legal proprietor or heir apparent of a huge and profitable corporation such as the Koch or Mars brothers of the USA. However, before their burgeoning business became a behemoth, the company must have had a straightforward charter and beginning.

However, to the tyro, nothing is as easy as pie when we are vying for a piece of the business cake. This is true when we are setting up our personal corporation. In addition to the government's legal fees, you have to pay the lawyer or paralegal his or her charges for filing and preparing the documents necessary.

You will be advised that there are advantages and disadvantages when the corporate die is cast.

The foremost advantage is that you are insulated from the avarice of zealous litigators except the government (they have first and inalienable right to your assets) and the bank by making sure you guarantee all loans.

The disadvantage is that you are subjected to double taxation: first when the corporation pays the tax, and then when it is distributed to the shareholders. The long arm of the government gets you both ways, whether you are coming or going.

Suffice to say, a gram of prevention is worth a kilo of cure as translated to metric. It may be a cliché but is still a sage rule to follow. So it is important to discuss this with your lawyer and accountant. To incorporate or not to incorporate? That is the question.

Business Development—Introduction

The importance of business has been established. You are now totally committed and convinced to dip your litmus paper to the business solution. You have the burning desire to commence and implement your newly acquired business philosophies and acumen.

The desire to enroll into a business enterprise had always tagged you on the shoulder before, but when you responded, your entrepreneurial GPS could not come up with coherent direction instructions. Who should we consult? Maybe we should get the answer from the horse's mouth.

If money could talk, it would advise us to develop a plan. We should be guided step by step with the proper procedures to minimize errors and effectively solve omissions.

The science of human development starts by the successful union of two (spermatozoa and ovum) cells. The process of mitosis increases the number of cells until a complete human being is formed.

Business development is similar to human growth. A simple combination of two diverging cells containing all the genes that carry all the traits and characteristics to complete a human being is nurtured with utmost care and attention.

The growth of the simple cells cannot be left for nature alone to simply take its course. Active participation in the care and maintenance is required to help in the prevention of future maladies. We should know what to do, such as a keeping to a balanced diet and exercising regularly, and what to avoid, such as the ingestion of alcohol and illicit drugs.

If all the necessary precautions and recommendations are followed, the chance of a successful birth is very good indeed.

The diagram below illustrates the different stages of development of a business.

Business development diagram

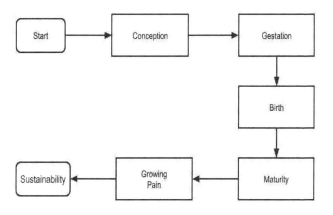

Figure 5

The Conception

If necessity is the mother of all inventions, then conception is the foster child. Once a business need is identified, the entrepreneurial mind is shifted into high gear, and the organizer starts to formulate a plan to take advantage of the business opportunity.

Conception is the process of forming or understanding the ideas that will form as the nucleus for our future venture. In the animal kingdom, nothing is born without going through conception or a similar process. In business, it is difficult to imagine a successful venture that did not start merely as a concept.

Yahoo!, a global internet brand, was conceived by its founders, Jerry Yang and Danny Filo, while they were studying at Stanford University. The concept was to be able to keep track of their internet interests. Their chronicle is fascinating reading, for their saga is a great business history.

Another interesting story is the one about the internet site YouTube. The need for sharing videos on the internet made the legendary company a pioneer and a pile of wealth. Google subsequently bought the business. It is now one of the most visited sites on the internet and has the highest bandwidth usage.

People come up with business concepts all the time. Ideas come from anywhere, any time of the day. They could be encountered at the beach, by someone knocking at the door, and yes, maybe tonight, according to Stephen Sondheim of the *West Side Story* movie. Look and you shall find is a proverb to keep in mind.

Once prosperity consciousness is adopted by the human mind, almost everything we touch or see is evaluated for its business potential.

If there is a possibility for success, the concept is analyzed further. The profitability of a concept is not obvious to everyone. This is exclusive to those with trained olfactory, auditory, gustatory, and optic nerves. Like a bloodhound, seasoned businesspeople can smell profit a mile away. They have twenty-twenty financial eyesight and hearing that resonates with the frequency of revenue oscillation. There are times when understanding a business's concept effectiveness is hard to grasp even when it is explained in detail.

Once a concept is adopted, like its human counterpart, it undergoes gestation.

The Gestation Period

This is the time the business zygote gets implanted. The preparation table has to be cleaned up, and the drawing apparatus is made available. It is time to compose the venture's flowchart of what to do and who is going to do it.

It has been said that from a small problem, a big one wants to come out. This is true with business concepts. A simple plan could have impediments that are difficult to overcome. Who could foresee the final tally of obstacles that have to be solved? The opposite could be true as well. From small ideas could come out big and roaring success.

If you are easily dissuaded by unwelcome advisers, you should nurture your ideas close to your chest. You could have bosom buddies coming out of nowhere dishing out unwelcome advice. This is why inexperienced people would not like to divulge the ideas to others for fear of ridicule. These critics somehow always know somebody who tried and failed miserably.

The truth is you need the input of others. Some people will make suggestions that will be very helpful, while others will likely be the devil's advocate. Your ability to make decisions will help you filter the advice, paid for or gratis.

The quality of advice is decided based upon your accumulated knowledge. The larger your reservoir of data, the less difficult it is to decide. The ability to decide is an important quality, as explained in sales and marketing.

Unlike the human gestation, we have full control over the development process. We can only influence it. Business gestation is totally decided and controlled by you.

You can even decide when to unveil your project, unlike human birth.

The Birth

The human embryo has fully developed and is ready for a grand exit. The birth canal is prepped; the stork is circling; the delivery is about to take place. Likewise, the business blueprints have been drawn, corrected, and revised. An enterprise is about to be born.

The flower shops are ready to deliver the bouquets of roses to celebrate and make festive the momentous occasion. Just make sure that your guest list includes people who are people of many words, for if it is true that you can say things with flowers, each of your laconic well-wishers may send just one rose stem. Your grand opening could appear to be like the gathering of the pessimist club, where members were encouraged not to attend.

The scent of freshly cut flowers in your establishment expresses your optimism for a prosperous business operation. Everything should look rosy, as the saying goes, but as with all learning curves, there will be moments that make you wonder if you made the right decisions.

All businesses undergo growing pains.

The Growing Pains

When it comes to hindsight, we all have twenty-twenty vision, a sage observation. It is true to life; it applies to businesses as well.

A fine carpenter will measure twice and cut once, but there will always be pieces that are short of expectations. Even with concerted effort to avoid mistakes, something can and will go wrong—Murphy's rule. Our game plan can have bugs hiding under a stone that was left unturned.

As in human progress, there will be the need for adjustments. The successful people are the ones who can trim their skills' potentiometer to accommodate present conditions.

The hallmark of an intelligent human being is the ability to be able to accept mistakes and adjust accordingly. All successful businesspeople believe that a profitable end justifies the troublesome means.

Maturity

The conventional wisdom is that if a business has reached the fifth year, you have survived the test of time. You have learned all you need to know. You have experienced all the facets of the business. You can let your guard down and can afford to go on an extended holiday.

In business, your competitors are the same as predators ready to munch on carrion. The difference is that in business, your competitors are not going to wait until your enterprise is given the last rite. They will administer it for you, and the earlier, the better.

Microsoft is a matured business. UNIX tried to challenge the dominance but could not soften up the hard-core followers of the software giant. Even IBM tried with OS2 WARP and had to withdraw from the race.

Microsoft, considering its obvious dominance, cannot sit on its laurels. It continues to offer improved versions for better performances and for privacy and security, a contentious issue especially on the internet.

Sale or Demise

"All good things must come to an end" is a maxim that no one can deny. We all have to retire sometime. The bones are tired and weary; the motivations are not there anymore. The ring spirit is beaten; the towel is about to be thrown to the canvas; the raised hands are not far behind.

You do not walk away from a profitable business. There are values in it, so you try recouping the maximum financial returns out of your life's work and then fade away like a true veteran. There are companies whose specialties are helping others to buy or to sell businesses.

To sell a business is not as easy as simply placing an advertisement; the interested party negotiates for the price and then closes the deal as in a real estate deal.

In real estate, you just make sure your house is commercially presentable, clean, and with all structural deficiencies properly fixed or concealed, and you are ready.

In business, the preparation for sale could be as long as several years before the market is ready to consider your enterprise. Profitability has to be restored if it is struggling; otherwise, only your assets will fetch any value in the auction sale.

There are tax considerations to settle. The structure of the deal is also important. Are you buying the whole business, assets and liabilities, or assets alone? Which one is better and why?

A Case in Point

You have just read how a business is started up to the possible ending. Let us examine the typical experience of a couple named Robert and Laura.

Robert Fray and Laura Record are a couple who work in a gourmet restaurant. Robert is the chef while Laura is responsible for waiting on customers. The pair are reliable and dedicated employees. Robert enjoys cooking. He has not seen a kitchen he did not like! Laura, on the other hand, is popular with the customers, whom she thinks are always right. The diner is owned by a Mediterranean native named Mario.

Bob and Laura love to entertain friends and have, on several occasions, catered for them. Guests are appreciative of the culinary expertise of Bob. Often, friends recommend that they should establish their own restaurant.

One day, Bob had a disagreement with Mario about changes in the menu that raised Bob's blood pressure to the boiling point. The argument encouraged Bob to seriously consider the couple's plan to own and manage their own bistro.

"We do everything for this man," they reasoned! Bob cooked and Laura served and controlled the cash flow. Thinking that they had the entire recipe for a successful venture, they decided to implement their dream of being their own bosses. "Let us see how Mario can survive without us," the couple confidently thought. With their minds made up, the couple started to cook a concept plan for a restaurant christened Bounty.

The gestation period did not take long because all they had to make sure of was their ability to maintain their lifestyle while they grew the business. Their bank savings account confirmed that.

Bob discovered a promising location near their house with plenty of prospective customers—ideal for Bob's culinary acumen. The rent seemed reasonable. The ten-year lease contract terms seemed agreeable; they issued a deposit check. A restaurant makeover artist did the plans for leasehold improvements; they were ready to fire up the construction start button!

Bob and Laura had a few thousand dollars saved for capital plus a loan to cover the rest of the leasehold improvements. A friendly neighborhood banker assisted them with a small-business loan to supplement their savings, and a promising restaurant got established! They were on their way to financial gluttony. Or so they thought.

The sweet dream started to be a nightmare when contractors did not deliver on time and on budget. To hire reliable personnel turned out to be a challenge, especially when they tried to get caring and hardworking people at reasonable wages. Attitudes do not always go in step with the demands. The growing pains could not be alleviated with heavy doses of analgesics.

But personnel demands paled in comparison with the others! A restaurant is the type of business that requires costly fixed expenses such as rent, taxes, and maintenance. In addition, there must be allocation for variable expenses such as the cost of food, extra manpower, and utilities. All of these had to be paid before Bob and Laura could declare a profit and pay management salary.

At the beginning, the business income could not sufficiently offset the variables, let alone the fixed expenses. Accountants call this negative cash flow. It is a condition when the deluge of the cash outflow (expenses) is more than the inflow (income). The business operation is gnawing at the reserve capital! The inevitable question is this: How long can the piggy bank survive this economic onslaught?

Owning and running your own restaurant business requires more than just operating a cash register and firing up the stove and oven. You could literally do the adage of the business: jumping from the frying pan into the fire.

In addition to serving and attracting customers, there are strings of tradespeople—government regulations for taxes, public health, fire safety inspectors, suppliers, and so on—to deal with.

If you are not fully equipped with business savvy, your chutzpah alone will not prevent you from getting fried in your own fat. The business could meet its demise before maturity. You may need a steady supply of antacids to survive the physical and financial toll.

You can see in the above story the misconceptions about having a business concern.

An entrepreneur is like the conductor of an orchestra. The impression is that he gets the accolades when all he did was swing the baton up, down, and sometimes sideways. He nods his head in time with the music. He cannot even conduct without glancing at his music sheet. How difficult is that?

For critics and pundits like Bob and Laura, making music is limited to any sound agreeing with the auditory nerves. All hum and melody have the same effects to an untrained eardrum. It would not matter if the maestro's conducting is sharp, natural, or flat. In the same manner, business amateurs like to play by ear. Learn as you go along—there are no tricks to learn, and anyone can do it.

Can a mechanic own and manage a car repair business? Absolutely! Does he have to be a mechanic to own and manage a repair shop? A resounding no! The responsibilities are different. However, it helps to understand the parlance and technicalities of your business.

To have a full appreciation of the management of a business, let us look at business more in depth. To accomplish this, we have to understand the way the revenue department of any government treats businesses.

There are two entities the revenue department is interested in. The first is the individual taxpayer, and the other is the corporation. Both have personalities. The difference is the amount of percentage the government department collects for tax purposes.

It is important to note that any country can and will collect taxes from anyone it considers to have income and personality. All registered corporations, incorporated limited companies, and the like are considered to have personalities.

If a corporation is supposed to have a personality, it must therefore have an anatomy: body, soul, and emotions.

Everyone has heard the words "limited company, corporation, firm, or conglomerate." This book is not intended to discuss the minute or big differences, especially their tax implications. There are plenty of reference textbooks one can read to understand and digest their different makeups.

The interest in this book is to understand the anatomy of businesses, big or small, limited, incorporated, or conglomerate.

The Brain

The expression "we have the same vibes" means our brains are vibrating at the same frequency or in resonance. We are thinking of the same thing, or our ideas are parallel. Is this simply an expression, or is there more to the phrase than meets the eye? To explain this phenomenon, let us try to understand the radio mode of transmission.

The heart of any radio or television station is the resonance box. This unit produces a carrier signal that vibrates at a set frequency allowed by law, 100 MHz for example, powered at a signal strength that will be sufficient for a distant receiver to intercept.

The sound or picture signal you want to transmit is added to the carrier signal by a process called modulation—hence the term *modulator*. The airwaves are full of signals with different modulated carrier frequencies. Every radio station is assigned a carrier frequency that identifies it. An example is when the announcer says, "This is your news station 105 on the dial."

At the receiving station, such as your radio or television, there is a resonance box that can be adjusted to a frequency exactly the same as the transmitting station. This is referred to as tuning in, when a device that has the same vibration frequency simply vibrates with the source. In the previous paragraph, it is 105 MHz. The receiver removes the carrier frequency by a process called demodulation. This leaves the sound or picture signal to be amplified for better sound and sight.

When a unit has the ability to send and receive transmitted signals via a signal carrier, it employs a modulator/demodulator (modem) to add and remove the carrier signal frequencies. Your computer is equipped with a unit that allows it to receive transmissions from the internet service provider.

So what is the significance of this lesson about radio and television transmissions? The reason is that everything in this world vibrates, including the brain. Theoretically, if you want to find out what is in the head of the chairman of the Federal Reserve Board, just tune into his brain waves for telepathic transmission. That way, you will know what is contained in it like the interest rates before everybody does. The problem is whether we know the vibration frequency of the secretary's brain. Can we email him to find out?

The great minds of business fill the airwaves with entrepreneurial signals. How many people succeed in intercepting these transmissions? In the event that you are successful in receiving these communications, can you understand and make use of these messages? It is unlikely, unless your brain is motivated and trained to utilize these vital ideas.

The brain is responsible for directing all human activities. Under its direction, we develop a plan, a road map to guide us to victory land. This blueprint of steps to follow will make it easier to attain our goals. Success depends on it! Business is like the species *Homo sapiens* we belong to; it has a personality.

"Sole proprietorships," "partnerships," and "corporations" are words used to describe the personalities of businesses. The government of the country where you live treats all business entities as if they have lives of their own. They have social standing. They have activities. They can sue and be sued. More importantly, they have to pay taxes on profits they derive from their operations. To the revenue department of the government, there is no difference between a business and a productive human being. Therefore, businesses, regardless of their forms, must have origins. They must have been conceived by someone! They must have gone through a gestation period, through some growing pains to then reach maturity. As in life, there are mortalities, and some are ailing. The health depends on how well the business was prepared and looked after.

An architect or an engineer will never commence on a project before all the plans and blueprints are carefully prepared and approved. The reasons are simple and logical. Architects are hired with commensurate compensation for their services. Results must be guaranteed, and workmanship carries warranties. It cannot be a haphazard affair! There are legal ramifications for errors and omissions!

On the other hand, when we decide to embark on a business venture, we are doing it for ourselves. We do not feel the need to prepare. We are answerable to no one! We do not see the need to acquire the necessary knowledge to successfully carry out the requirements and needs of the business.

We may have gone into a business activity because a friend or a relative is doing a similar and successful venture. We feel that we are smarter and more capable of doing the same thing. In other words, we are suffering from the syndrome that makes us believe that if he or she can do it, so can we.

That mistaken belief has been responsible for pouring millions of hard-earned money down the financial drain. The municipal sewage pipes are full of it! Your trash contribution is not welcomed.

The Plan

If you start not knowing what to do, you could end up not knowing what you have done.

This is a simple statement, but how many people are violating this elementary advice? Going into business is a very personal decision! It is very easy to start a business because we do not have to pass a qualifying examination. There is no need to be tested. It is easy to pass when you are the examiner and the examinee at the same time. Many people think that all you need is to have the necessary capital, and you are on your way to the profit land. This is the avenue lottery winners have traversed. It is a lonely road we call the boulevard of broken dreams.

There is a saying that goes like this: You give a fool $1 million, and he will lose it in no time; you take away $1 million from a wise man, and he will make it back in a short period!

To have a reasonable chance to succeed, what do we need to do? More importantly, what do we need to learn? Most of all, what do we need to prepare? What do we need to plan?

Remember even the best plans could fail. Here is a billion-dollar plan that failed.

IBM, in its effort to catch up with the desktop computers, asked its computer geeks and MBAs to draw up a model that could compete with personal computers. By this time, the competitors were far ahead, and PCjr, as it was then called, is now in the archives of old models of computers deleted from memory.

It is ironic that the personal computer market acceptance was due to the implementation of Microsoft's DOS operating system by IBM. Without IBM's blessing, who knows what the fate of Microsoft would have been.

IBM, thinking that the desktop computer would have the same fate as the fashion at that time, had no interest in the software that runs desktops. IBM made the mistake of just securing a license from Microsoft for the software used. Microsoft can also license other competitors of IBM without restriction.

Later on, Microsoft became the Goliath of the personal computer, eclipsing the original master, IBM. The PCjr experience did not teach IBM lessons because, later on, it developed a competing operating system called OS2 WARP, another fiasco waiting to happen, another set of nails for the proverbial coffin.

What will be the next success story? Somebody, somewhere, is working to make things happen. It all begins in the mind—an idea.

The Idea

People do not plan to fail; they fail to plan.—Anonymous

The following examples illustrate the need to have a clear understanding of the business you are about to start. Remember:

The best business ideas are free, but implementing these ideas, like lunch, is not.

There are stories that the initial concepts of successful businesses were drawn on restaurant serviettes. Business ideas were discussed at a lunch meeting, not realizing that they were gestating a plan that could make them wealthy beyond their wildest imaginations.

For some of them, the exercise was just to have fun, a force of habit maybe, but what a habit it is! Let us see some of them.

Two friends, while studying in Stanford University, had an idea of creating a program that would assist internet browsers to search for registered sites. Internet sites were indexed and ranked for display.

The service would be free of charge to browsers. Internet sites could pay for higher rank or pay to be included in the list of sponsored sites.

The latest revenue model is to share in the revenue from successful transactions. Net revenue is more than $1 billion per quarter! The simple idea is now a multibillion-dollar revenue generator. The partners are now multibillionaires. Larry Page and Sergey Brin are only in their thirties. They became known as the Google boys.

The lesson is that the two pioneers in the story may or may not have been aware of the magnitude of the business they started at that time. They must have believed in the phenomenal potential, but to what extent? We are sure they did not really care.

Today, Google is a juggernaut! It sends shivers down the spines of other giants like Microsoft. Google is able to entice the key employees of other companies to join it. At the time of this writing, Microsoft has not put up a competing search engine business that could threaten the dominance of Google.

On top of that, Google has so much cash for mergers and acquisition in order to expand its business or simply buy the new company with stocks. A case in point is the buyout of YouTube. The founders of YouTube got many millions of dollars for their initiatives. YouTube now is the largest user of the internet bandwidth!

Gates and Allen correctly predicted that personal computers would be on every desktop all over the world. The personal computer is now as ubiquitous as the television set. All these computers need operating systems appropriately named Windows and Vista.

Today, Mr. Gates is the richest person in the universe. He cannot possibly spend all the money he accumulated in several generations.

So he is giving away his wealth through his philanthropic window in his foundation. Unfortunately, we are not on the roster of worthy recipients, not even a free software.

One thing to consider is that if Mr. Gates was to give all his money of approximately $95 billion (2018 estimate) to the approximately two billion poor people of the world, the needy people could buy ten hamburgers at McDonald's.

Immortal gentlemen like Thomas Edison, Alexander Graham Bell, and Henry Ford used their inventions to create their business empires one idea at a time. We can fill up the pages of this book simply by enumerating names of successful inventors who went on to establish profitable businesses, big and small.

In the city where you live, there must be people who went on to establish a thriving business. It could be a small manufacturing company. It could be a cottage industry. It could be a mom-and-pop operation. Whatever the business they have established, you can always tell who they are in any given community. They are the employers, the so-called movers and shakers of society!

What are the reasons for mentioning these business greats and not-so-greats? In the next chapter, we will explore the evolution of business.

We know from previous chapters that money is just a convenient measurement of the stockpile of goods. It is the payment for the services we have rendered or goods delivered.

We also learned that business is the process of moving goods and services from the manufacturers and suppliers to the customers. Goods and services must flow. There must be kinetics! There must be organized deliveries of products and timely performance of services.

The process is the sum total of all the efforts put into the business. There are trials and tribulations. It goes through several steps. We can call the process business evolution. It will help you find your niche!

"I would like to go into business, but all the good ones are already taken" is the common lamentation of a frustrated businessperson.

Many postal workers sorting packages resent courier companies not because they are competitors but because they feel that the delivery idea was their concept. Unfortunately, these postal workers had no vision and did not push the envelope far enough!

The Evolution of a Business

This section will discuss the evolution of a business with the intent of learning the process so that your prosperity consciousness is given some road map to follow. This is to "awaken the genius in you," as Anthony Robbins said.

Businesses do not just pop up like magic. There are several reasons why businesses increase in number. Businesses are just like television programs—there are spinoffs. There are products that are new technologies that evolved from old.

Chester F. Carlson did not like the tedious job of making duplicate copies, so he invented a machine that employs a process called xerography—dry writing. He called his machine Xerox, the first copier to use ordinary plain paper. It is interesting to note that stalwart companies like IBM and GE and RCA rejected his invention until the Haloid Company, which later became Xerox Corporation, bought the idea to market. Though Xerox, as the joke says, did not do anything original, it revolutionized the reproduction industry. The rest, as they say, is merely a copy and history.

History did repeat itself. Xerox rejected the idea of personal computers when it came knocking at the door. The irony is that the Palo Alto Research Center (PARC) is owned by Xerox and developed the graphic user interface (GUI), which made the development of Windows. Windows programs, as we all know, made Gates and company many billions of dollars.

The computer is the wonder of the last quarter of the twentieth century. It is so novel that there are members of two generations ago who do not know how to use a computer, especially in the third world.

The Computer Bits and Bytes

The ubiquitous desktops, laptops, notebooks, tablets, iPads, and the like are all the offspring of the granddaddy of them all, the big mainframe. The undisputable patriarch is International Business Machine (IBM). IBM was not the first, but it became the most popular of the brands. UNIVAC was the first. IBM became so dominant in the sixties and seventies that the word "computer" was synonymous with IBM. IBM became so successful that it spent many hours defending itself in antitrust courts, accused of being a monopoly.

IBM mainframe computers are gargantuan even as of today. They are for huge applications and will provide computing services for years to come. Most of all, they are expensive, beyond the reach of small companies, let alone the common person! Something has to happen to make computers more affordable; after all, not all applications need the enormous computing powers of the big mainframes.

The first subdivision was the midsized computer, sometimes referred to as the minicomputer. PDP became the dominant supplier of the reduced-size system. The market responded favorably because there was the need.

During this time, technology has improved considerably! Components were reduced in size, prices were slashed, and the microcomputer was born! Entrepreneurs saw the opportunity that every desk in an office could have its own desktop computer. They probably did not even consider the household market. Computers in every home? "Preposterous," was the reply.

Computers started to invade homes. The computer subdivided again. There are the home computers, office computers, notebooks, and tablets. All of them have dominant makers and suppliers like Toshiba for the notebooks and HP for home models.

Every subdivision created new companies for the introduction and manufacture of new devices.

The computers need operating programs; peripherals like displays, printers, and disk drives; adapters like networks; supplies like disks and printing paper; and service engineers.

The internet application of the personal computer made it mandatory to individuals. It is not enough to have just one unit anymore. Different applications need additional PCs. Every day, new uses and applications are brought to the marketplace.

Many companies became billion-dollar businesses. Dell computers are an example, and so are Oracle, Intel, eBay, Amazon, Yahoo, and so on. The list is endless, with many additions every day.

Business opportunities are created every time a sector is born or new applications are developed. Somewhere in the nooks and crannies of this world is another computer geek with a venture idea. It is no longer limited to the Silicon Valley where the computer geniuses started this revolution with the technology industry. They are enviable in their direction; they are on the proper track.

The Automobile Track

If San Jose is the ground zero for technology, Detroit's auto manufacturing was the heart and center for transportation. All the big manufacturers soon had their head offices there. This is the Silicon Valley for cars, and Detroit has a big billboard that displays the count of cars rolling off of the assembly lines.

Ford Motor Company, with Henry Ford at the helm, is credited with inventing the assembly line technique. All manufacturers now employ this process.

The car industry became and still is a dominant industry in North America. The industry created many associated manufacturing and service businesses such as gasoline, tires, steel, and the like.

North American society revolves around the automobile. The car is an indispensable part of our industry and economy. When the car industries sneeze, the whole country catches a cold, as the saying goes. Countless businesses are dependent on the car industry.

If you are an inventor, there are many possible products you could make, from accessories to parts. Consider the case of Robert Kearns, inventor of the intermittent wiper blade. The major automobile companies used his invention but forgot to pay for the right or give Bob a royalty. He sued and got $30 million for his 1967 patent. His plight became the subject of a movie.

The roar of the automobile has not been silenced, but the speed is about to slow down. The automobile industry is being attacked on all fronts. The Environmental Protection Agency would like to eliminate the engine because of the pollution a car emits. Organizations like MADD (Mothers Against Drunk Driving) want to eliminate some drivers, while other organizations for responsible parenting like to eliminate the back seat.

Many business opportunities broke through because of the car industry. As stated many times in this book, if you develop your prosperity consciousness and apply the money principles advocated, you will find a venture that won't backfire or roll over. (Pun intended).

An enterprise associated with the automobile can take you places and is something to feed your cranial cavity.

Food for Thought

There was a time when it took seventeen people to feed twenty. Obtaining food is the number one priority for people. Next in order of importance is clothing, and then shelter.

With the introduction of modern machineries and technologies, it now takes three people to feed twenty. The food industry is the largest provider of work for students. Their compensation is referred to as "McPay" in reference to McDonald's, the most popular among the food chains and one of the biggest employers.

For trivia purposes, you may find it interesting to learn that McDonald's derives more income from real estate than food. They are investors extraordinaire of properties. If you see a stand-alone building with a McDonald's fast-food restaurant, they probably own it, with the franchisee as merely a tenant. They are experts in choosing locations. You will be hard-pressed to find a McDonald's site that closed because of a lack of business unless a Rambo wannabe used it for target practice.

The food industry has many franchisers. Burger King, Subway, KFC, and Domino's Pizza are example names of the operators. A franchise is an excellent way of starting a business.

There are advantages and disadvantages of franchising. The investment requirement is high in most cases. They also have strict requirements about the qualifications of the franchisee. They are interested in people who could successfully operate the business and are committed.

On the other hand, a franchise business model is established, and the growing pains have been experienced and resolved.

"The food business is excellent," these franchisers would readily claim. People have to eat. Look at the food court of any mall. All the shoppers are your potential customers, and they get hungry and thirsty from shopping.

When you answer the call of hunger pangs, you will notice that the food kiosks are highly specialized foods and service: pizza, hamburgers, salads, Chinese food, Greek food, Caribbean food, Mediterranean food, and so forth.

We prefer specialists because they can master their crafts compared to a jack-of-all-trades.

The Subdivision and Specialty

We saw in the section "Computer Bits and Bytes" the theory of subdivision and the businesses that spun out of an industry.

In the computer genealogy, Bill Gates could be the fourth-generation relation of Thomas Watson, and the Google Boys are family members by affinity. Subdivision is born when a business section expands and specializes.

How many divisions will a segment divide into? It is difficult to predict. Many started as a section of an established store. The demand for the product grew so that more space and attention were needed.

The pattern is emerging here that the demand must mandate the growth of a business. Here is a fascinating story.

The two biggest sellers of cooked chicken in the Philippines are roadside vendors of marinated chicken barbecue. This is possible because the traffic laws in the country allow these ventures to operate on the sidewalks. These food suppliers cannot be found in the shopping malls' food courts, where there are strict rules and regulations on fire safety and food sanitation.

Their clients are drive-by shoppers and pedestrians. They have very low overhead since the store space rent is cheap if not free. These are like the roadside vendors for fruits in North America during summer. Their customers buy and run, but their plumbing is nonexistent. Their water supply is just a drum beside the road.

Besides, they trimmed the fat from their operations; they do not use oil. This is an excellent and profitable "fowl" move. The vendors also added pork belly to their menus. Do not be surprised if they can influence the price of the commodity in the futures market.

The Storefront

Margaret Cho, a famous comedienne of Korean origin, bases her humor on the reputation of immigrants from Korea: that they tend to favor the corner variety store business. Maybe it is because people of Asian descent have the reputation of being knowledgeable in martial arts, which would deter would-be robbers.

If you are a person who wants to go into business but salesmanship is not in your blood (see chapter 5, "Sales and Marketing") or the vernacular is not your native tongue, you may be able to get by in business if you set up a variety or convenience store.

The business for sale section of any newspaper is full of stores for sale like beauty parlors, dry-cleaning businesses, shoe repair shops, newsstands, and lottery kiosks. There are three most important things to look for in addition to your other requirements.

1. The terms of the lease—is it long enough? Are the renewal rates reasonable?
2. Financial statements—are they sound? You may need an accountant to check the validity and accuracy.
3. Assets and liabilities—are you buying the assets only or the whole thing? If you decide to purchase the whole business, there could be surprises in the end.

If minding the store is not for you, you can join the millions of people promoting their products through the internet or mail order.

The Internet or Mail Order

If you have something to sell, and you do not want a store to look after because of the overhead, mail order or internet sales might be your best avenue.

Stores big and small also have internet sites to sell their products. We all know Amazon.com, the biggest operator of them all. eBay will be glad to assist you in the setup; after all, you pay a fee to be included on their site. You may have purchased this book from our site or from others who carry this product.

Mail order businesses' difficulty is caused by customers' great resistance to using credit cards online. The internet is cheaper to operate and wider in coverage. Just make sure to return their money if you are asking for deposit or prepayment and then cannot deliver. This is the law.

It is advisable for all students to learn how to publish an internet site. Many youngsters have this skill now, but it is mainly used for social networks. Few have business savvy to capitalize on this skill, but this is maybe a good thing. God knows we have enough junk mail already.

If people are not hawking something, they invite you to a business opportunity meeting, better known as multilevel marketing (MLM).

The Multilevel and Pyramid Schemes

You have seen some of the methods used to market a product. Which one is the most effective? That will all depend on your degree of business interest, capital, and ability. If you are like many of us, you have been invited to a MLM meeting at least once. Here is the account of a man whose MLM experience he will never forget.

A man involved in his fifth multilevel business proudly claimed, "I am working on my fifth million dollars." The audience was surprised because he did not look like a man of means.

"What happened to your first four?" a member of the audience asked.

"I missed all of them," he replied with regrets.

The Multilevel Chart

Monthly Income

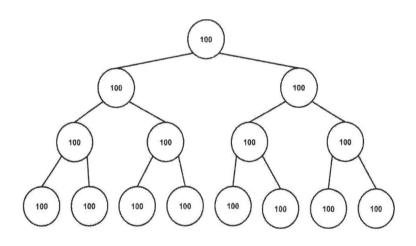

Figure 6

Multilevel marketing (MLM) is just one of the different methods of marketing a product. The system distinguishes itself from traditional business setups in that salespeople are independent operators or distributors. There is no employee/ employer relationship. Distributors are not paid salaries. They buy and sell products on discount.

Independent distributors do not earn commissions. There is a markup for each product sold to the customer. There is also a bonus for a set volume, which is like commissions in structure. All the different MLM companies give names to the bonuses like pearl, ruby, diamond, and so on.

Products sold by these companies are health and beauty products, household goods, insurance, water and air purifier, telephone services, pots and pans, vacuum cleaners, and the like.

The distributor can add to his or her income by sponsoring others to join the company (see above diagram). The theory is that each new member will generate income for you. The more people you invite to join your army of distributors, the more your income increases correspondingly. If you disliked math as a student, this will show you what you've missed. In just a short period of time, the presenter will lose you mathematically because the figures will boggle your mind. Multiplication is fun, especially when you are dealing with fictitious currencies in the amount only an MLM business can generate. As you sponsor more people, the higher your income becomes.

The theory is that sponsored members of your group "down lines" are going to assure the success of your organization. Your sole responsibility is just to provide motivation and momentum and, of course, their inclusion to this entrepreneurial group. Benefits will be generated even in your stupor or slumber, now and the future ad infinitum. The promoters even claim that they are earning whether they are in or out of this universe. Literally! They do not explain that there is a cut-off level.

Should a person you sponsored bring a new member, you also benefit, and so on and so forth. This process is repeated until your organization chart looks like a pyramid with you at the helm, seated comfortably at your MLM throne (see the diagram). The honest-to-goodness truth is that any product sold has manufacturing, distribution, sales, and marketing costs. Let us say the sales percentage is 40 percent; that is the maximum nugget regardless of how many aggressive sales agents are involved to partake in the MLM pot of gold. If you are at the bottom, there won't even be precious dust to cut with a microscopic knife.

This is the reason MLMs are sometimes referred to as pyramid schemes. MLMs have a similar operational pattern; therefore, it must be as devious as its close necropolis relative. As the saying goes, if it walks like a duck and quacks like a duck, it must be a duck!

If you Google a multilevel company, chances are you will be directed to a warning and most likely an unpleasant review advising you to stay away, as if these companies are epidemic carriers.

The blatant truth is that MLM operators need to sponsor as many as fifty highly productive people to truly make a substantial living. Emphasis is on producing. Sales are not optional like the promoters say but are conveniently disguised and vehemently denied. Do not worry; the guy above you will help you achieve that in a short time, is the deceptive advice.

All pyramid schemes are illegal, but true MLMs are not. MLM is a marketing scheme while pyramid is a method to scheme the market.

The difference is that in a true pyramid, no goods or services are involved in the business. Some devious operators try to get around this regulation by using a semblance product upfront, like a beauty product guaranteed to preserve your youth. You get your money with profits by enticing others to join. The law tried to keep up with these dubious operators by making dumping to be against the law. As the saying goes, the infractors are always one step ahead of the law, so beware!

MLMs are excellent methods to experience and learn about business. First, the capital involved may be negligible. Stay away if the amount required is more than one hundred dollars without accompanying products you cannot use. Second, motivation is the forte of these groups; sometimes, people at their gatherings sound and behave like people at religious services. You will notice that promoters are very convivial, and recruits are very aggressive with firm convictions that their newfound company will lead them to the financial bonanza that eluded them for so long.

The emphasis of MLM operation is recruiting. We learned in chapter 2 that recruiting, training, and retaining are very important to maintain a business. This is a desirable ability. But we will learn in chapter 5 that sales are the lifeblood of every business.

MLM operators avoid the word "sales" like a plague. They are not worth a second look. There is great effort to camouflage the pitfalls of the product. According to them, you can run a profitable business because your products or services are equipped with automatic sales wheels. For this reason, they do not train their distributors to follow the rules of salesmanship, which we will discuss in a later chapter.

Companies without successful sales programs will follow inevitably in the footsteps of the dinosaur or the flight path of the dodo bird. MLM businesses—like the kiwi bird of New Zealand—have all the customary anatomy of a complete bird. They even have wings, but they are not functionally designed to fly.

Something to Think About

This world is full of millions of business variables, so it is difficult to advise anyone on the exact steps one has to follow. Our parents and others can only guide us and show us the guiding principles with the hope that we can apply these theories for our own use; it is up to us to choose which one is applicable for us based on our unique abilities.

So far, your decision to enter the entrepreneurial world must be positive. But somehow, our ambition is telling us that there are a few more skills to acquire. Let us see what the next chapter will bring. Your decision to enter the entrepreneurial arena must be firm by now.

CHAPTER 4

Financing a Business

Any business's health is measured by the constant flow of cash generated by sales activity. As with the human body, blood circulation is the life-giving system. If blood flow is restricted, the physical condition is affected. If there is no movement of the life-giving liquid, fatality is not far behind or just minutes away.

In business, it is very important to have a continuous flow or transfer of paid goods and services. To guarantee a smooth movement for sales activity, there must be adequate financial support; otherwise the business will convulse and gasp for resuscitation.

When a business is established, the operational cash requirements come from the revenues generated by the sales activities and the negotiated line of credit (LC). The LC is the bridge financing that closes the gap between the receipt of revenues and current expenses. During startup, the supporting cash needs are taken from the capital contributed from the owner's savings and credit extended by the founders.

To finance the capital requirement of a business is the first responsibility of the founders. If money could talk, what would it recommend us to do?

To appreciate the importance of financing, let us consider the events of 2008. Whenever there is a recession like the one during the second half of 2008, even stalwart companies such as General Motors and Chrysler were begging for bailouts from the government. The United States and Canada were asked by the management of these companies to guarantee several billion dollars of loans to save jobs. These loans, if granted, are complicated and are beyond the scope of this book.

Let us see how financing is done, but first let us examine the dilemma.

The Chicken-and-Egg Syndrome

The proverbial question of which came first, the chicken or the egg, is similar to one in business financing. Consider the following scenario.

A prospective businessperson walks into a bank brimming with pride and confidence about his plan for a guaranteed moneymaking venture. He needs $100,000 to start a business, an amount he does not have. He learned about the small-business loan program of the government, where he could get a credit of 70 percent of the needed capital. He raised $30,000 using several methods like obtaining loans from friends and relatives.

He arranged for a visit with his bank manager, confident that after explaining his surefire idea, he would walk out with a check in hand.

Customer: I would like to apply for a loan, say $70,000.

Bank manager: What is the loan for?
Customer: To establish a business!

Bank manager: Do you have any collateral (e.g., bonds, stocks, real estate) worth more than $70,000?
Customer: Are you serious? If I had that much, what am I doing here?

Bank manager: Sorry, I cannot be of help this time, but please see us again when you have $70,000 worth of collateral.

To add insult to injury, the bank manager complimented him for a splendid idea and gave the man a pat on the back, which felt more like a punch to the solar plexus. The dejected man walked out of the bank with his shattered ego, feeling like a canine with his tail tucked between his legs, thinking that Bonnie and Clyde were justified for holding up banks. He felt like Lassie biting the bank manager in the leg.

There is no other dream-killing profession like the thankless job of a bank manager. They have been referred to as sharks, crocodiles with dripping tears, soulless people, and those who lend you an umbrella on sunny days and take it back at the onset of a drizzle.

Bank managers have a reputation that they love to beat people when they are down on their knees. Mr. Drysdale, of the television sitcom *The Beverly Hillbillies*, did a humorous portrayal of a typical banker, which we are sure is denied by officers of the bank.

In third world countries, the "Almighty complex" of bankers is even more acute. This affliction can only be cured by displaying domination. Considering the near usurious interest rates that they charge, the borrowers still beg the mercy of lenders.

If the developed country's bankers act like the third world, those moneylenders would go out of business in a hurry. Many transactions in the underdeveloped countries are above board, but an equal number of deals are consummated under the proverbial table.

Is the reputation justified? We all have our personal horror stories about dealings with our banks. Some are pleasant, but the rest are horrific tales. The reason we apply for financing is the lack of adequate funds to begin with. However, most bank managers will send you home feeling sorry for yourself and let you chase your own tail like a rabies-infected dog.

Failure to finance a business is undoubtedly the most important reason why people do not engage in any entrepreneurial activity, next to procrastination. Lack of capital is the number one reason why going into business is very intimidating.

So you are convinced that your idea will fly like an eagle. It feels like being given a license to print money. If only you had enough money to pay for the product development. If only you had enough capital to pay for the initial inventory.

Hold on! Isn't that what banks are in business for? Just walk into any branch. Explain your bright idea to the branch manager. You should come out with a commitment by the branch manager for the full amount you need to get your business going; after all, you promise to do all your banking with them.

Instead of putting a smile on your face after the interview, he or she tells you that your application will be forwarded downtown for approval. Notice that the manager said it would be sent for approval, not recommended for approval!

The downtown people had no opportunity to talk business with you personally. They do not know your business curriculum vitae, let alone your trustworthiness. They have to rely on the positive recommendations of your personal banker.

The manager should have said, "I will recommend your application for approval, but you have to wait for the final consent from downtown." If he did not give you his stamp of approval, chances are you are a dead duck. "Please do not call us, we'll call you" is the sympathetic but pretentious advice.

Before we discuss the loan application process, beware of the following.

If your intention is to get someone to pay the startup cost for a nominal fee and risk free, there is sad news for you. Unless you are an expert confidence artist (con man) and full of Irish luck, you are wasting your time.

Here is a personal story of a businessman worth relating.

> This is the story of how my wife and I turned $500 into a profitable business!
>
> In the city of Toronto in 1981, I was in my early thirties with two children, ages three and five. Our house, bought two years earlier, had an assumed mortgage renewed in 1981 at a 21 percent interest rate.
>
> My regular take-home pay was lower than our mortgage payment. My wife took care of our children full time and did babysitting occasionally. I called her a reserved womanpower. We had to stretch our budget like a rubber band about to snap and devise extra income to survive.
>
> My wife had to either find a regular job or go into business as soon as possible—and we had always wanted to have our own business. The desire had been building up for years. We had been peddling some goods and services on a part-time

basis so instead of looking for a job, we decided to seriously find a business. We felt prepared! Or so we thought.

In the '80s, Canada had labor shortages of nurses in particular. My wife and I immigrated from the Philippines, where many nurses came from. As a matter of fact, many hospitals in Canada and the United States employ many nurses from the Philippines.

Hospital staffing is always lower than the personnel required for full capacity. The reason for this is the variable patient census at any given time. The difference is filled by temporary nursing agencies like ours.

For a business, there is nothing more secure than having a Canadian hospital as your client because its budgets are backed by the government! Receivables are paid even when the economy is in recession or in deficit! Furthermore, people get sick regardless of the prevailing economic condition.

Armed with $500 in savings, we incorporated a business, secured the necessary licenses, knocked on the nursing director's door, and got authorization to supply nurses based on demands.

Since we were the employer, we had to pay the nurses' wages every two weeks, but the hospitals paid every month or longer. On top of that, government deductions and matchings had to be remitted every month without fail. With the business capital depleted by the setup cost, how could we fund the growing biweekly payrolls?

With AAA creditors, we should have been able to get a bank to bridge finance the receivables. Unbeknownst to us, in 1981 only a few bank branches dealt with business loans.

Most of them dealt with consumer loans, such as loans for cars, homes, and appliances. Receivables as collateral were areas some managers would not touch with the proverbial ten-foot pole.

We had an impeccable credit rating, so we were able to borrow a small amount based on a personal loan, but it was not enough.

Had we known the principles of financing, our shoes would not have had the holes from pounding rough pavement. By accident, we stumbled on a manager who taught us the ropes before the twine strangled us. That would have been a pity because we have a profitable and prosperous business. An adequate line of credit was established.

The business took off as anticipated. It has been our cash cow and source of pride and enjoyment, thanks to the financing supplied by the bank.

The irony of the experience is that the more retained earnings we have, the less we needed the bank's money to continue the business, but our line of credit increases every year. This is like the rainforest asking for more humidity.

What are the secrets of financing? Before we take a look, readers must be warned that it is possible some bank managers will not understand and sympathize with you. Maybe it is beyond their responsibility, but they will not admit the limitation or will simply distrust you as an applicant.

Do not let that discourage you! As long as you are confident with your plans, you will succeed in the end.

The Financing Cycle

Finance is as precious as a diamond. It is not surprising then that the process of qualifying for a loan is equated with the valuation of the prized rock. The five *C*s for diamonds are color, cut, carat, clarity, and Cartier (as claimed by their employees); these are the basis for value for the tough rare carbon.

For financing a business, the five *C*s are illustrated in the following diagram.

The Five *C*s of Financing

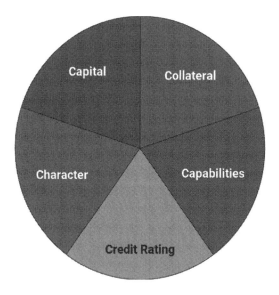

Figure 7

Credit Rating

The diagram in figure 8 illustrates the process of a typical bank transaction. The depositor makes savings like a guaranteed investment certificate (GIC), and the bank will in turn lend the money to borrowers. This transaction happens every minute of the day around the world. Most of us have done it; we do not think much about it.

The bank arranges the transactions. The bank assumes the lending risk because interests are guaranteed, to the depositors. The banks make excellent profits even when the economy is on the downturn, and even with large loan losses.

Bank Money Flow Diagram

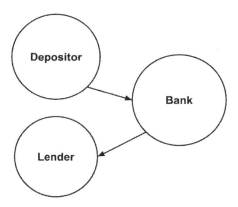

Figure 8

The diagram illustrates the invisible wall that isolates the depositor from the borrower. For this reason, the borrower's guilt for unpaid loans is alleviated by the fact that the remorseful feeling is directed at an institution instead of an individual. In doing so, those delinquent borrowers are unknowingly damaging their credit ratings, their best ally in times of economic rainy days.

Credit rating is the catch-22 of the borrowing world. If you do not have a history on which to base your credit rating, you cannot borrow, or the amount you can borrow is very limited. No lender will touch you with a ten-foot pole if your credit history has a failing grade.

We put this as the top requirement because this has been the least understood and most abused of the five *C*s. The value of our credit rating is not realized until we become victims of our own negligence. Credit is a valuable asset because we do not always have the necessary cash to back up our projects. That is where a credit facility is important. But first it has to be established. Credit cards are the best way to earn a credit rating. If you pay your bills on time, there are no interest charges unless you borrowed cash.

Credit rating is the point system called on to decide if a person or entity is financially responsible to justify the extension of credit. Like the grading system in school, it is used to determine our eligibility to climb to the upper class. A failing mark is *raison d'être* for disapproval.

Some people think that they have debt problems when their problem is their reluctance or failure to pay. People with good credit ratings are the ones who give the highest priority to their loan payments when they have cash. The ones with bad credit ratings do not care about loan payments but love to borrow regardless. All of us have a relative or friends of that nature.

The stamp of loan disapproval is like a loudspeaker in the minaret proclaiming to the world that we are guilty of distrust, sentenced to be stoned for neglecting our monthly principal and interest payments.

Credit ratings are an important asset, more valuable in fact than money in the bank. Credit is like a reserve army ready at a moment's notice to pay our business suppliers and ready to provide our business needs and allow operation without interruption. To maintain a good credit rating has no cost, while a line of credit carries a monthly fee.

It is important to maintain a healthy credit rating so that we have available funds to activate when the time is appropriate. Businesspeople or companies will have credit from you in the form of unpaid invoices. You expect prompt payments, so you should pay too—quid pro quo.

Delinquent loans are the cancer of the credit business. Unfortunately, the cancer-cell-killing ability of chemotherapy cannot be applied to offending borrowers. Until then, we all contribute indirectly or directly to the loan loss provisions.

It is a pity because it would ease the capitalization of business.

Capital

There was an advertisement on TV about a boy applying for a job in a department store. The manager asked why he was looking for a job instead of playing hockey somewhere. The boy replied that he was applying for a job precisely for that reason; that is the vicious circle of business.

How many times have you heard the statement, "You need money to make money"? That is like informing a blind man that he will be able to see if he can personally read and follow the instructions written on a piece of paper, no Braille allowed.

Every now and then, someone comes to us and tells us the following tale.

> I have this fantastic invention idea that will make us rich beyond our imagination. I am including you because I like you, and you are like a brother to me.
>
> My idea requires $50,000. If you put up all the development costs, half of the profit will be yours. In addition, I will do all the work, and you will just be a silent partner.
>
> Believe me, if I only had the capital, I would not be talking to you.

What is wrong with the above scenario?

First, our inventor wants us to pay for all the development costs for an unproven idea. It is very doubtful that J. K. Rowling got an advance pay for the first Harry Potter book. She could do that for her succeeding projects after a successful launch of her first book but not until she had proven herself to be a bankable winner with a magical bank account in the Potter Road branch.

Second, he asks us to contribute to all the financial needs of his operation. If the project does not work out, all the losses are yours. Is it because he has some doubt himself that it will work?

Most business loan applicants believe that the idea or invention is theirs, so there is no need for them to contribute to the capital. This is the same rationale that employees do all the work while the owner gets all the profits.

Henry Ford had a patent for a horseless carriage (motorcar). His investors put up all the capital, and their thousands of dollars invested paid millions in dividends and stock appreciation. This is a special case because people had seen him drive a prototype, and everyone wanted one. Ford prospered and bought out the original investors. When the motorcar became popular, the down payments for orders financed the manufacturing cost.

To prepare for business, one must start by accumulating assets that could be cashed in or used as collateral. The advantage of the latter is that the asset is merely kept safe by your lenders as collateral.

Collateral

Collateral is the item of value that the lender can use as a security for the loan. It must have a market value no less than the loan applied for. Collateral is the oxymoron of the lending business. Why would any sensible person go out and borrow money and then leave a security that is as valuable as or more than the loan itself?

Here is an anecdote.

A man walked into a bank and asked for a demand loan for $5,000 and left his Rolls-Royce as collateral. "This is the best loan I ever saw," said the manager. The loan is only a fraction of the worth of the car, so the investment is as safe as money in our vault. Two weeks later, the man returned and paid the loan with interest. The manager asked why the man had returned so quickly.

The man explained that he had to make an emergency trip to Europe, and there was no secure place to park his favorite car. He said that the bank would make sure to take care of his car and would not damage its investment. Besides, the interest the bank charged was lower than the parking rate of a garage he knew, and his reckless son could not take his friends for a ride.

In the anecdote above, the bank manager loved the high ratio between the collateral and the loan. This was his fail-safe security. For this reason, mortgage-free real estate is the preferred collateral, especially if you are only borrowing 75 percent of the appraised value. Commercial value is usually higher than the assessed price.

Assuming that your credit rating is excellent, your capital is within limit, and your collateral is acceptable, there are still other considerations, such as your ability to pay the monthly loan payment—in a word, capability.

Capabilities

Capabilities are the capacity and ability to carry your debt load. This is the vital requisite of lending. Lending institutions have a yardstick to determine one's ability to afford the cost and principal payment for a loan. The exception was the man we met in one of the business fundraising dinners for the hospital.

A man, another supplier to the institution, sat at our table and told us he is contributing to the osteology studies of medical students.

We asked where he imported the human bones from, and he indicated that these remains came from India. Our curiosity got the better of us, so we inquired where he stored these specimens. Without missing a beat he said, "I keep them in our basement and some in my closets." All of a sudden, he looked like Grandpa of the Munster family.

He did not look at all like Bela Lugosi or Vincent Price; because he looked very benign, that money manager would grant a loan to this client even with skeletons in his closet as long as he has healthy gross to debt ratio.

If Money Could Talk

The gross to debt is the total of monthly debt payment to monthly income, which is the measure of your available cash to pay for your credits. From 30 to 35 percent of monthly stipend allocated for debt services is a healthy ratio favored by lending institutions.

The subprime fiasco of 2008 was caused by the lax enforcement of this vital borrowing requirement. It was not ignored, but the enforcement was not rigid, and supporting documents were not thoroughly verified. It was not necessary because the institutions responsible for arranging these mortgages sold these funds to others, thereby insulating themselves from the subsequent fallout.

Another caveat for loans is the process called borrowing from Peter to pay Paul. The following is an illustration.

Vicious Circle of Credit

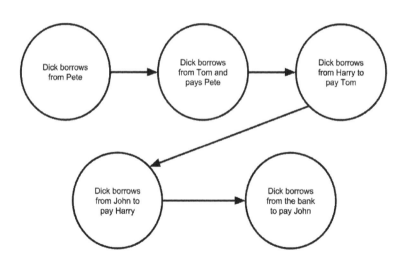

Figure 9

As shown in the illustration, Dick borrows from Peter to pay Paul. When Peter demands payment, Dick borrows from Tom and pays Peter—and so forth. Dick never gets out of debt by repeating this process, simply by financing debts with another round of borrowing. The procedure is never ending, which will not liquidate the loans. As a matter of fact, Dick is always looking for lenders. This is referred to as "kiting."

This is effectively the same when you pay only the minimum payment required on your credit card. Your loans never get liquidated. You are perpetually in debt, which reflects on your character as a credit risk and as an unreliable person. An 800 number calling could be from a credit card company trying to increase your debt allowance, especially if you pay your credit card regularly with just the minimum required until you are drowning in debt.

Character

The debtor must make the lender feel secured by way of collaterals, enough capital, business capabilities, and a clean credit history. But most of all, to have a successful relationship with the bank, the clients must gain the trust and confidence of the bankers. Simply stated, you must have the cunning talent of a confidence artist applied beneficially and honestly. You must gain their trust and belief in you.

Lenders like to trust you; after all, credit is the financial engine that drives the car industry. It is the solid economic foundation of the housing business. Without credit facilities, the economy would move at a snail's pace or maybe stagnate.

Didn't the government bail out the bank just recently considering the abuses they committed?

Credit: The Lifeblood of Our Economy

In North America, the economy revolves around the housing and automobile industries. An important barometer of the health in the United States and Canada is the number of housing starts and automobiles produced.

Houses and cars are mostly financed by credit, so if credit is tight, the sales of the two backbones of the economy suffer. The consumers of America also depend on credit for most of the household items they buy. Credit cards are more readily available than cash.

Most of our junk mail is from credit companies offering lines of credit indicating that cash is just a preapproved application away. These lending institutions are very aggressive in enticing you to mortgage your house, savings, and even your soul, if you have one. They are very nice until you default on your payment, and then they send their collection agency squad with baseball bats who will track you like a hound dog capable of a nasty bite. Thanks to call display, you can buy yourself some time until you get a summons from the courts.

The Right Bank

If you have ever watched any sport and had no clue about the rules and intricacies of the game, chances are you could not follow and enjoy it, let alone participate in it. Take the game of North American football. A novice might wonder how they could call it football when the players only kick the ball at the start of a ball possession and after every touchdown. To add to the confusion, the descriptions of the players are quarterback, running back, and so on.

An aficionado of the game will be able to tell the expected functions of every player, while to an untrained eye, it looks as though they are just running aimlessly and arbitrarily passing the ball, praying the Hail Mary to increase their odds on catching of the ball—hence they christened the desperate maneuver the same prayer, merely for good measure.

If you think banks and lending institutions are like that—one bank is as good as the other—you are sadly mistaken even when they carry the same name. That is like believing that any garage can fix your Ferrari, Lamborghini, or Rolls-Royce. Different bank branches have specialties that are directly related to the manager's qualification.

The reason is that all banks are not equipped to handle just any transaction you throw at them. They have favorite accounts too. The unfortunate thing is that if you go to a branch that cannot grant or understand your request, they do not necessarily direct you to the suitable one. Make sure you knock on the appropriate door; otherwise, you will enter a bank of confusion, not concessions to your application. You can tell if the head honcho is forwarding your application "downtown" and is merely passing the buck.

This brings us to the documents you need to bring with you during the application process.
The Supporting Papers

The Credit Application

The chapter 8 checklist discusses these issues in more detail and gives some examples. One thing to keep in mind is that all bankers love paperwork and documents. Your chances for approval are greatly increased if you prepare them properly with care.

The credit application gives the banker the very first impression of you, so it is no surprise that this should be the starting point of the loan process. It is very similar to a job application in format but differs in the purpose. Be sure to include all the relevant information that could help in evaluating your request.

The Projections

The projections are the assumed summary of your future business expectations. You use a spreadsheet program to chart the monthly progress of your business for the first year. You can use the same program to map the yearly projected increase of revenue and profit for the next four years. This will attest to your confidence about your business that it will take off like an eagle or need a space to run in preparation for a successful takeoff like the Andean condor.

Predicting the weather is more scientific and accurate than your projections. The weather bureau has equipment to measure the wind speed and clouds. In making projections, all you need to do is define the expected monthly increases of revenues and expenses in your spreadsheet program and voilà! Here come the neat expected answers using a formatted chart.

When it comes to the projections, you could have said to your banker, "Your guess is as good as mine." Though the result is similar, the process is more useful, to the banker at least.

The documents you submitted are written evidences of your capabilities and belief in your business, for you may be asked to provide proofs of the rationale of your projections. The significance is measured monthly, especially in the first year of operation.

If you exceeded the submitted projections after one year, you will have no trouble renewing your line of credit. But if you missed, you better have a letter from your ophthalmologist to explain why you misread the financial target marked for your eyes only. The projections are not random, plucking figures from thin air, but are a mirror image of your capabilities and honesty as a businessman.

The Financial Statements

The financial statement (see samples in chapter 7), especially for a business at the starting gate, is merely a record of the financial activity during startup. This is more evident in the following paragraphs.

The Balance Sheet

The balance sheet is a snapshot of the company that enumerates in detail the values of the assets belonging to the business, the liabilities owed, and the owner's equity.

Though the balance sheet is supposed to be an accurate valuation of the assets and liabilities, the real market value may not be the same. For example, a piece of land may be entered in the books based on the purchase price, but the current value may be higher or lower, depending on the present condition.

If a popular resort or amusement park is constructed or under planning, the value of land owned may be more than the book value. However, if there is a plan to build a correctional facility nearby, the valuation is definitely different.

Normally, there are no hidden assets, but you could find them in the liability section. Examples are potential litigation obligations, tax liabilities, and warranty misrepresentations.

Other Sources of Financing

Venture Capitalist

As a rule, venture capitalists will not entertain requests for financing from companies that have not proven to be viable businesses. Besides, their approval process is not as simple as those of lending institutions. For these reasons, this book is not going into the details of the process of employing the services of a venture capitalist. Besides, you are better served by consulting the experts in this field.

Suffice it to say that companies such as Microsoft, Google, and Yahoo were all financed by venture capitalists before they went public but were not necessarily at the starting gate during formation. These businesses were initially financed by well-to-do benefactors.

Wealthy Friends and Relatives

At the risk of being branded as a social climber, if your roots are not in the who's who register, you'd better cultivate friendship with families of means. If they trust you, they could be your best allies when you establish the next Microsoft, Google, Facebook, or Yahoo.

The emphasis is to be able to financially support your bright business ideas through creative financing. The ability to finance is synonymous with business ownership. In the financial statement there are two entries that are of concern for a business owner: the capital and current expense. The former has something to do with the assets of the company while the latter has something to do with the day-to-day expenses. Many companies met their demise by neglecting these concerns.

As we said, brilliant business ideas are given the last rite when they could not be supported financially. Creative financing is the forte of a seasoned businessperson.

CHAPTER 5

Sales and Marketing

Next to public speaking, sales can be the most dreaded activity for any person to do. It is very intimidating and uncomfortable for most of us. It is potentially a humiliating experience. The experience could be filed under the most embarrassing moments folder of our lives. As a matter of fact, some of us would rather go for a root canal than do a sales presentation. Cold calling, as they say in the business, is the process wherein the salespeople knock on doors or call on strangers for presentation. We are familiar with solicitations by phone such as "Avon calling," an MLM representative, or a telemarketer selling duct cleaning services.

These overseas telemarketers are aggressive and will call at any time of the day, especially at mealtime. Even a do-not-call list is overlooked; after all, how could you sue an overseas disturber? How much negative feedback can a person tolerate? Apparently infinite for those jobless citizens of third world countries with terrible accents.

These businesses operate on the batting average principle. The expectation of success is a very low turnout, but it is acceptable for their purpose. It is just like throwing a bowl of spaghetti on the wall. Few will stick, but that is expected.

If Money Could Talk

The definition of "sell" is to deliver or give up duty, trust, or loyalty, especially for personal gain, and to develop a belief in the truth, value, and desirability.

With a definition from an authority like the dictionary, it is no surprise that the majority of us abhor selling. There is no delight with the activity it instructs us to do. We avoid it like a plague—for the connotations of the word "sales" are phrases like "selling your soul to the devil" or "selling your grandmother for five cents."

There are many psychological and personal reasons why salesmanship is so intimidating. The sales experience compounds our fear of failure. The rejection phenomenon could empty the mind of any coherent thoughts and paralyze the vocal cords from vibrating.

If money could talk, what would be its recommendations to make us feel at ease and enjoy the sales process?

If we understand that sales are the lifeblood of all businesses, we have no choice but to overcome the fear and pain of selling and have fun with the process instead. Sales are like bitter medicines. We ingest these elixirs, but the astringent aftertastes linger on. Therefore, we need to desensitize ourselves, conquer the phobia, and alleviate the side effects. We suggest doing this by understanding the following truth.

There is no business, big or small, thriving or struggling and extinct, that is not involved in the sale of products or services. As stated in the previous chapter, business is the flow of goods or services. Without this movement, the business name should fill in the obituary column of the newspaper.

Goods and services must change hands or ownership as fast as they can. It is the speed of movement of goods and services that constitutes business health. Sales and marketing are the circulation, the life-giving system, of any business. The sales activity determines if a business is alive, on life support, gasping for air, or dead.

Accountants define businesses as a cash flow. This confirms that cash will not flow unless goods and services are sold.

Many of us have been invited to join a multilevel business. The invitation is usually described as a benign gathering wherein the guest speaker is merely going to share an investment opportunity (a euphemism for a business that requires you to sell). Upon arrival at the venue, you will notice the congenial greetings, tight handshakes, and hearty smiles. These are the hallmarks of an evangelical assembly. You realize then that you are in the wrong place. Like in a turbulent airplane, you begin to familiarize yourself with where the nearest exit is for a possible escape.

During the meeting, the speaker will avoid the word *sales* as if it is a tongue twister or pretend it is a lapsus linguae. There's a great effort to disguise the selling activity as inconsequential. For a person experienced in business, that is a revelation contradicting all enterprise theories and exposing the amateur status of the promoters.

The following is a sample experience of a former recruitment candidate.

> One day, I was invited to a multilevel recruitment meeting by a friend whom I owed some favor. The speaker started to draw circles with dollars in them. The circles in increasing numbers were stacked one on top of the other, resembling a triangle, hence the reference to a pyramid.
>
> At the very bottom, the numerical figures amounted to $24,000. This, the speaker proudly proclaimed, could be

your monthly income! He then asked if the audience could use the bundle of cash. Like a religious chant, everyone responded in the affirmative. He kept repeating the question in a crescendo. The audience stepped up the decibel of the answer to the delight of the speaker, who was confident that he had captivated the audience.

When the euphoria settled down, I asked the speaker how much sales I had to produce to be entitled to the hefty $24,000 a month. The multilevel guru assured me that there was no such requirement. All that was required of me was to recruit members to join the organization.

"It is not clear to me where the compensation would come from," I reiterated. "I look at the bonanza as a commission, so I expect to have put a larger amount in the coffers of the company. He offered to repeat the presentation to clear the financial cobwebs in my mind. I assured him that it would not be necessary.

Where would the company get the promised compensation if I had not produced any sales?

The answer was that these are rewards for signing up innocent people to blindly cheer their business. It was not necessary to generate revenue for the company he represented. All I needed to do was simply to round up gullible people to confine in the company coral. No production or selling was required.

The person seated next to me figured out my query and echoed my doubts. That's when the speaker and his entourage flagged me as the devil's advocate. Before the group decided to escort me out of the room like a baseball fan who interfered with the ball, I decided to keep silent as a courtesy to my friend who had invited me.

The next time you are invited to a business opportunity meeting where the organizers claim sales are not involved, you now know that it is just a waste of your funding time. It does not make any business sense. You are better served by enrolling in the school of legerdemain. Opportunities are opened simply by uttering the word *abracadabra*, and the Sesame of business opportunity will open. Could it be a box owned by a girl named Pandora?

They make money the magical way—just wave a wand. They make the mint printing press obsolete and a waste of time.

Selling is the circulation system for any business. Inventories must be sold or services rendered. Like the human body, circulation is what keeps us alive. If our circulation is weak or faltering, we need to be on life support and maybe in the hospital. If it is stopped, we are clinically dead. So is business.

Just remember the following:

> Money equals goods and/or services.
> In business, goods and/or services must flow.

Selling may be a difficult and an unpleasant job, but somebody has to do it! That is the responsibility of the salesperson, who is courageous enough to brave the promotional storm. What is he or she made of? What makes him or her tick?

Marketing

If you know the difference between a warranty and a guarantee, you probably can differentiate sales from marketing. Like the former, there is a fine distinction between the two. Where does one end and the other begin?

For our purposes, we define marketing as the ideas to promote products and services like packaging, while sales are the actual exchanges of goods or services. Many books deal with the subject. We will limit our discussion to the relationship of sales and marketing to the establishment of a business.

The obvious and first question to be answered is what product or service should be the cornerstone of our venture. What are the criteria for the decision to engage in a particular service or type of goods?

Marketing is the horse before the cart in the movement and smooth flow of products or services in the world of business. It is the first item of interest that has to be considered because the success or failure of our venture depends on the cleverness and effectiveness of the marketing plan.

The decision of what kind of product or what nature of service we want to provide depends on the following unassailable laws of marketing.

It Pays to Be First

If you have a product or service that is new in the market, you do not have a competitor; hence, you can establish a lead. However, you will learn in the section about sales that you have to create a need for your product or services. Since your business is not known in the marketplace, it may be costly to educate your customers, the buying public. Do you have the budget to pay for the expense of disseminating the need for your business?

A disadvantage is that once your market is in place, there is a possibility that another company with deeper pockets could enter the race and displace you. The advantage of being first is that people remember pioneers more readily. We remember the first president of the United States but may be confused about who is second, let alone the third, fourth, and fifth.

To be first does not mean that your product or service is so new that nobody has heard of it. It could be a new segment of the industry as a result of subdivision. We know what happened in the computer industry.

Once you have decided on a product or service as the cornerstone of your business, you will have to give it a name. Choosing a name is difficult at best.

What Is in a Name?

The choice of the name of the business is as critical as determining the nature of the business. Companies or individuals who can afford to may run a competition or employ a professional company that specializes in creating names, but if you are like most of us, you give it your favorite moniker.

Some company names are descriptions of the services they provide, like Microsoft (software for microcomputers), National Cash Register, and the like. Others are the names of the founders, like Dell Computers, Mars Bars, Metro-Goldwyn-Mayer, and so forth.

There are successful companies whose names are from foreign languages like Google (Russian) or acronyms like DYLEX (damn your lame excuses) or YAHOO (yet another hierarchically organized oracle).

Regardless of the name you pick, remember that potential customers have to be educated to know you. If they do not remember your name, at least get a phone number that will spell your name like 1-800-FLOWERS.

Andrew Carnegie, in negotiation with another steel magnate, agreed to a merger because the name of the new company is the magnate's surname.

Some of the memorable business names are Colgate-Palmolive, Gillette, Xerox, IBM, Google, Boeing, and so on. The names of these companies are synonymous with the products they make or services they provide.

This indicates the company's specialties as well. Boeing signifies airplane, Colgate is synonymous for toothpaste, so with Gillette for razor blades, Xerox for copiers, and Google for search. When a verb is coined in your honor, you know you have made it big time.

Specialize

We have seen in the evolution of business that enterprises usually subdivide. Every subdivision results in the introduction of a new segment ready for another split.

Browse the television channels, and many of them are specialty channels dedicated to certain types of programming. There are sports channels for golf, football, baseball, and the like. You will find news, science, travel, space, history, discovery, home and garden, food network, and so on.

There are many stores with single types of products like shoes, sports paraphernalia, or greeting cards, just to name a few.

Perception

The most effective marketing tool is to create a perception of being the best in the field. If you think of a product such as television, a brand like Sharp could stand out as the best flat-screen TV because its advertising says, "From sharp minds come sharp products."

Once the perception of being the most reliable is established, it sticks to the minds of customers as the truth regardless of the veracity of the claim.

As stated, a clever marketing scheme makes the job of selling much easier and more effective.

Sales

Lease contracts are signed with all the t's crossed and the i's dotted. Machineries and inventories are set up. The storefront is clean, open, and ready to receive customers. You will now realize the importance of salesmanship. As a businessperson, you are the first salesperson of your company. As a stockholder entrusted with the responsibility of affecting the flow of your goods or services, you have to apply all you learned about salesmanship. Let us explore what these lessons are.

If you think you have the congenital enthusiasm of Og Mandino, a successful car salesperson, consider yourself lucky; you are ready to drive your customer happy with a new toy and take him or her for a ride. You are made up of DNA that does not need the selling virus to infect your genes. You do not have to train your promotional butterflies to fly in formation for aerial blitzkrieg. Selling to you is a cinch. Selling does not intimidate you. You are as cool as a cucumber. If all the people in the world were like you, there would be no need for gastric antacids and ulcer medications.

Are Salespeople Made or Born?

Who are the best salespeople? You must have heard the expression that the best salespeople are the ones who could sell a refrigerator to an Eskimo. Consider the following anecdote.

A cunning salesperson felt the need to prove his selling prowess to himself. "Wouldn't it be wonderful if I could actually sell a unit to any resident of the Arctic?" he challenged himself.

Our star salesperson boarded a plane to Alaska to search for a potential Eskimo customer and got him to order the latest model of refrigerator, complete with water and ice dispenser. Satisfied by his abilities and accomplishment, he went about his business of looking for prospects. He found an Arctic dweller named Nanuk, and sold him the food preserver.

A couple of months later, the salesperson followed up the sale with the customary service call to find out if his customer was happy with the product. The salesperson also asked the Eskimo to recommend a friend or a relative.

The Eskimo explained that overall, he was happy and satisfied, especially when his wife finally developed the knack of chopping the block of ice to fit the ice tray.

The selling process starts during the formation of the company. In the previous chapter, we discussed the process of product and service selection based on the principles of a sound marketing plan.

The sales process is an art that can be learned, practiced, and perfected. Different people will utilize different procedures and techniques, but most sales presentations follow a predetermined format. This is sometimes referred to as a boxed presentation. That is how all product training manuals are constructed.

Sales successes and failures are a direct result of the inability to apply effectively the three basic steps of sales. But first, you have to arrange for a rendezvous with the prospect. This step is the tornado before the storm. Let us test our survival ability to weather the business hurricane.

The Appointment

To be able to make a sales presentation to a prospect, an appointment must first be made. Most sales presentation meetings are arranged over the telephone. The rejection rate is highest at this level. If your guts are not made of steel, the telephone receiver gets heavier after every failed call.

How many rejections can you tolerate before you throw in the towel and call it quits? The success rate of making appointments is very anemic indeed. There are proven techniques for an effective appointment call. The following is a typical telephone call.

> Salesperson: Hello, Mr. De la Joya. I am Manuel, better known as "Pac Man." I would like to demonstrate to you the latest punching bag. This is new in the market because it screams corresponding to the strength of your punch. Would you be available on December 12 at 11:00 a.m. or 2:00 p.m.? If not, I can make it on the fifteenth at the same time.
>
> De la Joya: I am not available at those times. As a matter of fact, I am not available at any time.

Salesperson: How about on the twenty-seventh of this month at 10:00 a.m. or 3:00 p.m.?

You will notice that Manuel did not ask to be given permission to make a presentation; rather, he was making De la Joya choose a convenient time. This is known in the magic circle as "misdirection."

Making appointments operates on the principle of what is called in the baseball world a batting average.

A batting average is the result of a semicomplicated formula that is not really important for this illustration. Let us say a player has a batting average of .300, which means this baseball ace successfully got to first base three times out of ten. Putting it another way, he has a success rate of 30 percent.

The reward for this ability is a multimillion-dollar contract. You can see that you do not need to have a Midas touch all the time. A 30 percent success rate is excellent, especially if the return is in the millions of dollars.

Once you have mastered the art of making appointments, you merely have to learn the craft of salesmanship.

The Sales Process

Create the Need

A great business practitioner, when asked what business a person should get into, said, "Go find a need and fill it."

Most businesses are established to satisfy that very need. We go into the food business because people have to eat. We set up a car repair shop because we are sure that cars will break down. Automobile towing services wait in highway entrances imploring Satan to create havoc so that there is a towing need in the hope that this vulture is the closest to the accident scene. If you cannot invent the need, get an ally; even Lucifer himself. For example, *La Cosa Nostra* initiated the need for security by starting the catastrophe themselves; then the syndicate offered their protection services.

The above examples are cases where people realized the needs and did not need to be convinced of the necessity to buy the products or services offered. To further illustrate this point, if you are a car dealer salesperson assigned in the showroom, the browsers there are in need of cars. And diners who walk into a restaurant already have the hunger pangs secreting gastric juices in their stomachs.

The necessity to create the need for the above cases is duplication to what nature has supplied. Necessity has imbedded in their minds the desires.

However, if your products or services are new and unknown to prospective customers, people have to be made aware of what your products or services can do. Potential users may not understand what benefit they could derive from it. That is the first responsibility of a salesperson.

There are no hard and fast rules for how to create the needs. It all depends on the circumstances and what is effective for you. A word of caution: if the need is not properly established, and a successful sale is not made, the susceptibility of product returns are very high. Impulsive buyers upon reaching home could easily change their minds; after all, they have no idea what to do with the product they just bought, or they realize they could have gotten a better deal somewhere else.

If you have returned a product in the big retail stores, you will witness firsthand the long line of customers who realized that they do not want the product because they do not need it after all or, worse, that they actually do not want it.

Sales manuals for products and services always commence by clearly defining the needs, whether the salespeople realize them or not. Product knowledge is paramount at this point because if you as a promoter do not know the benefits of your products and services, who would?

You have to be creative. You have to demonstrate clearly the benefits of your product and the paybacks of your services. If the need is firmly established, you can go to the next step. How can you make the customer like your products and services?

Make the Customer Want It

When a prospective customer has agreed that there is a need for your product, *ipso facto* this person must like your product or service, right? Not necessarily: it does not follow that he or she wants it. A hungry person's taste buds may not agree with your recipe. A short man may not go for elevator shoes though the footwear may help in his acceptability with the ladies. Want and need could be as far apart as New York and Los Angeles.

People are creatures of habit. People do not want to be told. They do not want to be sold. It is insulting to be told what to want. Dale Carnegie in his book *How to Win Friends and Influence People* said, "The customers convinced against their will are of their opinions still."

It takes all your ingenuity to sway a person to appreciate your side of the sales presentation. You have to set in motion your power of persuasion without the customer feeling that he or she has been used.

How many times have you heard people say that they need something like an umbrella to protect them from the ultraviolet rays of the sun but will not buy a parasol because they need a tan. Deciding between health and beauty is difficult at best.

Let us assume that your prospect has realized the need for your product or service, and by your power of influence, you determine that the desire to buy from you is evident in his actions. Could you then finalize the deal?

What you have done so far is educate the buying public. The thrill of the sale has been building up like a jet plane taking off, whose engine is screaming in crescendo. What is there left to do? What is the next step? It is the most difficult to master in the art of the deal.

Going for the Close

The proverb "you can lead a horse to the water but you cannot make him drink" is most appropriate in the sales presentation. The bronco simply would not even imbibe a drop of your dripping pitch.

A person may say to you after your presentation, "I need your product or services! With God as my witness, I want it too!" Then you hear the most discouraging word that would make your knees buckle. You say to yourself, "Good Lord! All I have accomplished so far was mentor the person." The dreaded word is *but*.

Close but no cigar! The bills will remain unpaid; the planned purchases are put on hold.

"Close," in sales parlance, is what determines whether you will have a feast or a famine—whether you have wasted your time or will celebrate in triumph.

Of the three steps in sales, the closing technique is the most difficult to master. Successful salespeople are masters in the art of closing a deal.

To learn the art of closing a deal is to have the charisma of Gandhi to make a sales prospect affix his or her John Hancock on the dotted line. Watch the process employed in the car showroom.

Salespeople who have mastered the art of listening and talking at the same time are in the top echelon of the selling game. While making the presentation, the words and actions of the prospect must be analyzed at the same time, a difficult job to do, especially for a novice. Like a cat stalking its prey, the salesperson knows when to activate the burst of speed to capture the prey.

Why is this important? It is because of the fact that at the end of the presentation, the prospect may decide to reject your offers for a reason or reasons. Is this prospect telling you the truth or saying what is nice to hear? The difference cannot be dichotomized with a fine-toothed comb.

When someone tells you, "I do not have the time or money," is he or she saying, "I am not willing to give you the time of day or a dime"? You cannot succeed by addressing the wrong issues. White lies are preferable to being a noble hypocrite.

Expert salespeople know that the most intimidating part of the sales process is affixing the signature. Remember that signing on the dotted line is a legal commitment. This is the reason why the application form is made ready even at the onset of the presentation.

You do not want to scare the customer by the act of searching for the dreaded sales document.

The length of sales apprenticeship is proportional to the time it takes to learn the art of closing. When you learn the sales techniques, it is hilarious to witness the sales drama unfold before your very eyes. An innocent question such as "Which part of the house do you like best?" is called a closing sign when selling a house.

Closing signs are probing questions that signal to the salesperson that it is time for the coup de grâce. This differs from person to person, employing a wide range of emotions and actions.

Women have a definite advantage over men. This is because it is harder to say no to smiling ladies, especially with demure eyes pleading mercy. It may sound cavalier, but it is true.

Lessons According to the Experts

Here is a salesperson's tale of the sale.

> The very first book that I bought outside the mandatory reference books for school at age fifteen was *How to Win Friends and Influence People*, by Dale Carnegie.
>
> The lessons I learned about human relations completely changed me. I started to remember and call people by their first names, for it is the sweetest sound in the world. It is difficult for many people to memorize them, but you get better in time.
>
> The pretentious feeling cannot be hidden, for during our unguarded moments, our gestures (outward expressions of

our inward intentions) will give it away. The lack of a smile indicates tense feelings and apprehension.

Do Not Argue

There is a piece of wisdom in sales that states, "You may win an argument but lose a sale." Business is not a popularity contest. Defending your pride is not the objective of a sales presentation. It is to move goods or services, for being without this flow could hurt deeply your pocketbook and business.

Sage advice from experts is that the best way to win an argument is by avoiding it. Steer clear of the temptation to prove that you are right. Think of how to spend the money you make out of the sale if you need some comforting thoughts.

Words to Avoid

If the pen is mightier than the sword, as the saying goes, then the tongue is sharper and more tenuous than a freshly sharpened katana. A sharp tongue may cut your throat, a Chinese proverb says. Sound travels faster than the blazing speed of a knife-wielding martial arts expert.

In sales, deals are made or broken by what was said by the salesperson. So what are some of the words to avoid?

The top of the heap is *convince*. It is true that you are there to sway the prospect's thinking to your side, but to be blatantly told we are being convinced is contradictory to our intelligence and repugnant to our common sense.

Second is the very reason of your presence, *sell*. Nobody can stand being convinced; to be sold something without our initiative is even more repulsive.

To start a presentation by saying, "I'm going to *convince* you to buy this product I *sell*" has dropped your vending average to the negligible.

The hallmark of a successful salesperson is to be able to adjust his or her presentation in an instant. At the end of the presentation, people will give reasons for not purchasing a product or service.

Service, Service, Service

Unless your business is a store that sells items worth one dollar each, your warranty ends at the cash register. Most customers expect excellent service from retailers.

"Your satisfaction is guaranteed or money refunded" was a successful slogan for a former giant retailer in Canada that lasted for more than a hundred years. Customers love the idea of being able to return any product without giving reasons for doing so. The only requirement is that the product must be accompanied by the original receipt. There must have been sufficient merchandise returned that they finally closed their doors.

Walmart has the same policy, and it is dominating the marketplace. In addition, the stores offer low prices and claim that their people make the difference. This is very excellent for a store that started as nickels and dimes, even if you consider the effects of inflation.

An excellent business practice is to create a pool of customers who patronize you over and over. This in not only a good policy; it is survival.

Marketing, Sales, and Money

The ability to move products or services is what constitutes a business. This chapter confirms the importance of marketing and sales. If money could talk, there would be an emphasis on these items.

So for the sake of wealth accumulation, sales and marketing must be adopted in our list of desirable traits and capabilities. They are the gatekeepers who could open the doors to financial bliss.

CHAPTER 6

Motivation

We live in a very complicated world bubbling with problems that are as complex to solve as the Rubik's Cube. The most imperative problems to unravel are financial problems because they affect our lives in the most critical way, from food to clothing, shelter, and recreation. If you are limited to one word to differentiate prosperity from paucity, what would that declaration be?

If money could talk, the word would be *motivation.*

Our parents and teachers must have stated at least once in our lives that the reason we are accomplishing nil is due to a lack of motivation; therefore you must have written your goals with disappearing ink. Unfortunately, nobody provided us a minimum dose of stimulus elixir that would awaken our dormant enthusiasm to accomplish anything of value.

There are millions of elementary and high school dropouts for the simple reason that they have no idea why they are attending school. If given the choice to play their video games or do homework, their interest is obvious: do what is more fun regardless of future ramifications.

Few youngsters realize that one day they will be adults with Atlas-like responsibilities. When that day comes, and they are unable to cope with everyday responsibilities, they just simply blame society for failing them, believing they deserve a lifetime of support to compensate for their negligence.

Why is motivation difficult to understand and acquire? For motivation to gain acceptance in our minds, it must pass through two tightly shut doors with failsafe security.

The Conscious and Subconscious Minds

A normal human being has five senses. All outside stimuli are received and interpreted by the conscious mind (e.g., pleasant smells, cacophonous sounds, bitter tastes, etc.) Then all of that information gets stored and compiled in the subconscious mind, assuming that the conscious mind allowed the information to enter in the first place. That is the first barrier (door), and we all know what a closed mind is; the guard is stricter than the Swiss soldier of the Vatican.

Unfortunately for some people, their minds are more open to unnecessary, illegal, unpleasant, and appalling things than sensible ideas. Somehow virtuous, decent, and moral deeds are harder to accept.

As we grow older, there is more reliance on our instincts, meaning we are utilizing our subconscious minds more. The computer adage "garbage in, garbage out" becomes important because had we been feeding the subconscious mind a steady diet of refuse, that is precisely what we will get. On the other hand, had we been nourishing the subconscious mind with prosperous ideas, we would live a flourishing existence.

The diagram below illustrates the typical income versus expenses pattern. Depending on where you end up, black (savings) or red (deficit) determines the action needed to be taken.

The Income/Expense Diagram

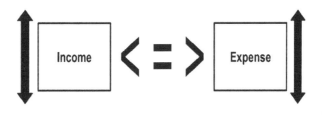

Figure 10

Incomes > expenses = savings
Incomes < expenses = deficits

If your monthly bank statement indicates a positive balance, you belong to the minority group. You have developed your prosperity consciousness very well and deserve to be congratulated.

On the other hand, your options are unpleasant if your income is less than your expenses. You have a choice between tightening your belt or augmenting your income. If you do not, every day takes you closer to the offices of debt arbitrators or bankruptcy court.

Some people in any environment can live in style without a care in the world. They are the ones who are free from debts or family crises and obligations. Their only concern is to have hearty meals with high nutritional value and no contamination problem. Happiness to them is a nongrowling digestive system. Life is simply continuing the prosperous life they set for themselves.

Clothing and shelter are not their priority; after all, fashion is just making a statement without saying a word, and they are taciturn by nature. They have business appointments to keep and social rendezvous to make.

For most of us, God seems to have given us sight just to torment our sanity. Competition is an everyday activity. We want to keep up with the Joneses, hoping that they can't afford anymore as soon as we catch up, but the problem is exacerbated when the Joneses refinance or have deeper pockets.

How can you avoid turning white with anger and have a tanned complexion instead? This is a very difficult task, especially if you live in a third world country where God seems to have forgotten and abandoned you. Everything is difficult to come by. What can we do?

Even just for the sake of complacency, you must believe that you have enough talent and ability to make it on your own or at the very least to take charge of your own success; after all, it is inconceivable that God created anybody to be nobody.

To rely financially on others is limited by the mercy and patience of your benefactors. They say that all good things must come to an end, so it is just a matter of time before you are at the end of the line.

How should one commence to acquire the prosperity consciousness?

Desire

The difficulty with desire is that it is an internal stimulation. The incentive emanates from our guts. That is why the Hebrew word chutzpah describes a person with the bravery to try to do new and unproven things.

Most motivations are externally induced, which means they started from our parents, teachers, and then our environment. We respond to the senses of sight, smell, hearing, touch, and taste! But how could we motivate ourselves to respond to the call of prosperity, especially when the action needed is confusing and difficult?

A terrifying sound could scare us half to death, and whatever audacity is left can be taken away by a frightening sight. We react automatically to that. We get hungry passing by a bakery shop when bread is baking in the oven, polluting the air with an appetizing aroma!

You could taste the sweet nibble and feel the warmth of fresh, piping hot bread. The desire to eat is triggered, but it does not necessarily motivate you to reach for your pocket and purchase a loaf or two.

Why? Is it because your desire to eat is not strong enough? Is it because you are anorexic, not sufficiently hungry, or do not want to spoil your appetite for a later meal?

People with weight problems cannot ignore the invitation because the desire to eat overcomes the resultant physical problem. Their minds are programmed to respond to any appealing sights and aromas. That is not necessarily true for all people.

To spring into action, you must have a very strong and persistent desire to do or get what you want regardless of the impediments.

Many people would say, "I like and desire it, and God knows I need it, but I cannot afford it." The mind is excellent in rationalizing too.

A businessperson called his company DYLEX, an acronym for "damn your lame excuses." It sounds and looks like a vanity plate!

He may have chosen the name to remind and motivate him during those uninspiring moments and when the going was tough!

There are books written dedicated entirely to the word *desire*. They are all inspiring and can help in understanding the causes of procrastination. You will like them for sure if you are able to find the time!

As stated at the beginning of this section, desire is something that nobody can serve to you on a silver platter. The trick to this predicament is to eliminate the conjunction "but" in your lexicon. You will find that all rationalization, excuses, and defenses will disappear like dust in the open air. When you have sufficiently filled your bucket of motivation, you will need to acquire the knowledge to implement your plans.

It is our hope that this book gave you reasons to desire more wealth and, more importantly, that you have started accumulating all the knowledge you need to carry on.

Knowledge

Whoever said that "investment in knowledge always pays the highest interest" hit the proverbial nail on the head.

Do not make the mistake of believing that knowledge is equal to formal education. There are long lists of successful people who have not been awarded the sheepskin diplomas before their lucrative businesses were established. Michael Dell, Bill Gates, and Jeff Bezos are just a few.

It is interesting to note that many of these baccalaureate-deficient pillars of business did not stay diploma short for long. Cash-strapped universities will easily grant them doctorate degrees to expunge their names from the list of dropouts who succeeded in making a mockery of the importance of the institutions of higher learning.

Have you heard of the incoming university president being advised by the board of chancellors? They told the newly appointed head honcho this:

"Be kind to your students with grades of A and B; they may come back to become professors someday.

"Also, be kind to the ones getting C and D; they may come back and donate a new wing for the university."

One of the founders of Research in Motion left his studies during his undergraduate work and later went back to build a new addition to the school.

Successful people are not necessarily the ones who know the answers to questions like "What is two plus two?" but the ones who could put two and two together.

Knowledge acquisition costs can be expensive, cheap, or outright free. It all depends on where you got them. The following is an anecdote of unknown origin, but it illustrates the moral of this lesson.

A job applicant who passed the written examination with excellent marks impressed his interviewers even more when the candidate stated that he learned his superb skills from Yale.

We have an Ivy League candidate in our midst, the panel thought!

The congratulatory handshake was about to be extended when the interviewers asked, "What do you prefer to be called, Jim or Johnson?"

Jim responded, "Yim or Yonson, either one is fine with me."

The above anecdote demonstrates that copious work-related knowledge is an excellent qualification regardless of whether you are captivated by the learning experience or learned in captivity.

To function well with any given task, one needs skill and knowledge. The skill can be congenital, but the knowledge is definitely learned! Simply having knowledge is not enough. That is the reason why university professors are not always the richest members of society.

The president of a university who spent his whole life on the campus, first as a student, then as a professor, subsequently as dean, and then president, finally quit his tenure to work for the company they used for case studies.

There is a piece of wisdom that states, "Those who can, do; those who can't, teach."

The importance of knowledge cannot be overemphasized. We should not waste the time spent in university because this time serves as the stepping-stones for our future.

University gives us the starting point. You have to expand on it, as Mark McCormack wrote in a book titled <u>What They Do Not Teach You at Harvard Business School</u>. Most of his successes as an entrepreneur were not learned under the guidance of the Harvard faculty but through fighting his way in the corporate jungle bare-knuckled. Mark had a long list of clients that are big leaguers in the sports world, such as Tiger Woods, Bjorn Borg, and so on.

To think that you are fully armed with knowledge after university to tackle the world is to wake up staring at reality disappointed. Who or what is at fault?

Here is a story to prove the point as related to us by a Rotary Club member.

> One of the charities we give to as an organization is a scholarship grant to deserving high school graduates. This award is given to the high-achieving student during a dinner where his or her parents are also invited.
>
> During the dinner, I was at the same table with a family who immigrated from a developing country. I asked the father what course the son was going to take.
>
> The father proudly said, "I do not care what my son is going to take as long as he is top of his class. Being the highest guarantees him jobs and opportunities unavailable to others."
>
> A father like that is the nightmare of many students. I could only sympathize with the son. The father's belief that a top science student is automatically the best rocket scientist is blasting off with the wrong propellant.

This type of thinking is typical of families from the third world. Education is the passport to an improved lifestyle regardless of one's ability to apply that knowledge. A degree is mandatory for any type of well-paying job but is not the only requirement.

Board examination results in developing countries indicate the candidate with the highest marks, equating him or her with the smartest and most intelligent. Usually, he or she is the know-it-all kind of person, the E. F. Hutton of the investment world; when he or she talks, everybody should listen.

If this is true, then economic standing will mirror the academic marks, which everybody knows is a fallacy. The ability to apply that knowledge is more important, and that is beyond the reach of any teacher. Here is a sample.

The superintendent of the US Air Force Academy in Colorado remarked to one of the graduates prophetically that he would not amount to anything. The superintendent based his observations on the academic marks awarded by his professors.

This student became a skilled flyer, the first pilot to become an ace in the Vietnam War. As a reward for his aviation proficiency, he was subsequently appointed as the youngest superintendent of the famed fighter school at Edwards Air Force Base. His aviation talents are found in the blue yonder while his academic marks are down to earth.

During the appointment ceremony, the ace whispered to the former superintendent his observation during his school days. The academy superintendent abashedly said, "I was hoping you would not remember."

The first thing to do in your difficult quest of wealth accumulation is to fill your head with appropriate knowledge you will use in accomplishing your goal. If you got it from school, then you do not have to travel the extra mile of acquiring it. The Google boys developed their search engine at Stanford University, a convenient place, especially since the school provided them with superb facilities.

George Lucas of the *Star Wars* films got his start at the University of Southern California's School of Cinematic Arts. University education is very important and should be taken advantage of, especially if you are able to. But what about the ones who cannot afford to go to the best schools, or any school, for that matter?

If Abraham Lincoln could acquire an education largely without formal schooling, so can we, even if we are not vying for the US presidency. When you have defined what you want to learn, look for the best place to get it and then assess the cost of acquisition. After your mind is full of know-how and information, respond to the director's command of "lights, camera, and action."

Action

Biorhythm is the internal barometer that determines our bodies' functionality. There is a belief that this is dependent on your birthday. The veracity of this claim is questionable at best.

However, there are times when we feel down and lack the enthusiasm to do anything. What would prompt us to respond to life's movie director's call to action?

Oh no! Another motivational talk, you might say! There is an army of motivational speakers: Anthony Robbins, Donald Trump, and Joel Osteen, just to name a few.

What is motivation? What does it do for you?

Motivation gives you the appetite to eat but does not give you the food. It does not even give you the ingredients to cook your own menu!

A nurse in a nursing agency got hit with the motivational bug. She decided to attend a seminar chaired by the king of reality shows, Donald Trump, now the president of the United States. She and her husband paid $500 for the privilege of hearing the immortal words of the Donald. They hoped to decipher the formula of affluence from the authoritative lines of Mr. Trump, who promised to deliver in person his sermon on the hotel convention mound.

The audiences and the critics were disappointed. All they heard was the rift between Donald and Rosie O'Donnell. To add insult to injury, the listeners were asked to pay for the books and tapes. The books are as difficult and confusing to decipher as the Rosetta stone explaining the theories of wealth accumulation.

The problem most of these attendees experienced upon arriving home was that they did not know where and how to start. All the words they could remember from the seminar were just a group of unintelligible words. They could not make sense of the lessons, let alone implement them. Also, President Trump has rhythm that's hard to emulate and has flamboyance to match.

The following is a true experience related by a disciple of multilevel business.

Feeling confident he had stumbled on the magic formula for wealth accumulation, a man we shall call Roy wanted to spread the financial gospel. He prospected a neighbor named Jack.

Before Roy could make his opening pitch, Jack started to recite a litany of his financial woes: his house and car could use some repairs, his kids needed support for school, his wife was complaining about the household budget, and so on.

Roy, remembering that need is the starting point of salesmanship, felt that his work was cut out. Roy assured Jack that a solution was just one house away! If he would only attend the meeting in Roy's house the following Thursday, he would be supplied with surefire answers to his dilemma.

Like a good neighbor, Jack attended and attentively listened to the plan. Jack followed the circles that looked like a pile of logs stacked one on top of another until the presenter had a diagram that look like the work of an Egyptian master necropolis builder. The only difference was that buried deep in the structure was a mother lode; it is just for the digging!

The following day, Roy visited Jack to get his reactions and impressions about the presentation!

Jack, with an excited voice and an act like he had just won the lottery, said that he gave his problems a second thought. They were not as bad as he thought they were! All his concerns were swept like dust on the vast tundra.

This book is arranged so that the required knowledge and necessary desire is discussed and established first; that way, you will have a leg to stand on and will not be working in the dark. There is no pretension to claim that all concerns have been properly addressed. This is just a starting point!

The Unfortunate Environment

The diagram at the beginning of this chapter 1 illustrates an ideal condition where there is an income to speak of. There are many cases, however, where there is no income or money available to spend even on basic necessities.

We may live in an environment that is predominantly poor, and our neighborhoods play a very crucial role in shaping our destinies. Despair and the acceptance of it stare us incessantly in the face.

Paul Newman, the dean emeritus of method actors, became a bona fide performer with his portrayal of Rocky Graciano, the former middleweight champion of the world.

Rocky's environment in New York City was the breeding ground of despair and hatred of the system, especially to the affluent people of Manhattan or Long Island who are just a subway ride away.

Rocky's life was changed unwittingly by the benign force of the system he lived in! It took a long time for Rocky Graciano to capitulate to the pressure to reform to a better and productive lifestyle, but as luck would have it, he did it before the worst had happened, and he lived to enjoy it.

On top of the personal benefits that Rocky derived, Paul Newman's portrayal of Rocky's career got Paul's roaring acting career started; Robert Wise earned a bundle from directing the movie, and MGM made a fortune from ticket sales.

The events unfolding in the nooks and crannies of this world are readily available to most of us thanks to modern communications such as televisions, the internet, radio, newspapers, mobile phones, faxes, and the archaic mail.

This speed of transmissions keeps us informed! At the same time, it makes us aware of the progress going on around us that we cannot be part of, especially in the art of accumulating wealth and accelerating our arrival to desperation land.

We feel like packs of hungry hyenas salivating at the sight of a cheetah with a fresh kill. We want a share of the same bounty by hook or by crook.

But hooking a catch requires patience and ingenuity—virtues we are not willing to use. The crooked method is oftentimes preferable even if we have to fight for it, possibly getting injured or fatally wounded in the process.

Full understanding of what money is allows us to be part of this feast but only if we are motivated enough. That is what money would say if it could only talk!

The following information may be useful to reinforce our motivation.

Sample Land Distribution

Let us examine the following data of an overpopulated country whose citizens believe that they could solve the financial predicament only if they have enough land to assist their plight.

    Land Area: 3.2 million square kilometers
    Population: 1.06 billion (2008)

Assuming the government distributes every square meter of land to the entire population, that would be about two thousand square meters for the whole population.

Two thousand square meters of land is enough for a reasonable house. The moral is that hoping for land for prosperity will not solve all of our economic problems, especially when there is no capital to build a residence, let alone the maintenance.

CHAPTER 7

Checklists

To secure a credit facility is advisable, even when you have available cash on hand or wealthy relatives. The reasons are that you never know when you will need money beyond your cash on hand, when relatives will sever ties with you, or when you will want to leverage your business.

Credit facilities are buffers a businessperson can use in times of sales and invoice collection slowdown or cash shortages. This chapter will discuss briefly the procedures and documents needed to apply for loans.

Business loans differ very little from personal loans, especially during startup. As a matter of fact, there may not be any difference from the standpoint of the credit lender, regardless of the personality of your business.

When registering a business, you must decide on the personality or form of your business. Do you want a sole proprietorship or a corporation? Which one is better and more advantageous for your needs? Your lawyer can best explain the preferred method, so our discussions will be limited to liabilities and their effects on credit facilities.

What would money tell us if it could talk?

The main advantage of a corporation is in the area of public liability. The owners can hide behind the corporate shields when there are financial claims against the corporation, unless the issues in question are credit and taxes.

Taxes are the responsibilities of the corporation, but in cases of defaults, the government goes after the owners; there is no way to escape that. The long arm of the law can break any defense we put up like a hot knife slicing butter.

In cases of credits, lenders like banks usually require the owners to sign personal guarantees that in the event the corporation cannot pay back its loans, the shareholders are left to carry the load. If your idea is to put others on the hook in the event your bright ideas get dimmed, think again and think wisely.

Therefore, it is incumbent on the novice businessperson to make sure of the business profitability and to operate legally and honestly. To go into business is the mantra for this book. It is understood that there are many problems you will encounter along the way. It is for this reason that before embarking on any enterprise, our personal lives must be above board and free from adverse financial black marks.

When you first apply for a business loan, you have zero balance on your venture's credit rating. As a matter of fact, your business is merely a legal excuse for granting you a loan, especially if you are taking advantage of government programs such as small business loans.

You will soon find that all the probing questions are about you and your loan history. Your excellent credit rating score is your passport to credit land. Bad marks will haunt you like loan ghosts of the night. You have to make yourself a promising candidate and worthy of credit. If you are, then it is easy to provide your lender with your borrowing and business history, which is an important document in your submissions.

Business Credit Application

This is the curriculum vitae of the business owners, outlining their experiences and enterprise outlooks. All lenders will want to know the applicants' previous involvements and accomplishments. For veteran entrepreneurs, this is routine, but this could be a dilemma for an apprentice without a record of similar or exact experiences. What should one do?

There is sage advice: "if you do not have a virtue, assume one." This could be the occasion to list the assets you always wanted to have but were afraid to mention.

Like a job application resume, the contents are the items you deem necessary for the bank to know you better. It is best to keep personal information such as your religious affiliation (unless the lender favors a particular group whose members are given preferences), age, sexual orientation (this is obvious for some, but do not tell unless asked), and moral convictions.

The lists of information you need to include are purposely omitted, for this is your first exercise in decision-making. You must choose what you think is important and relevant to show you can own and manage a business. Also, your lending institution may have its preprinted form.

The other documents, however, have to follow a strict format. Financial statements must adhere to the generally accepted accounting principles (GAAP). This is for ease in reading and understanding.

Sample Projection

A projection summary is the owner's vision of the business's future and goals (market share) that the owner expects to accomplish. The projection is like the income statement with entries tabulated monthly in the first year and then yearly for the next five. It details the expected income and expenses to produce the goods or services. Most importantly, it must show the profitability of the enterprise. Remember these are all educated guesses about the progress of your business.

This form can be laid out in any spreadsheet program where you make assumptions about the progress of your business. Numbers and Excel are excellent programs that any computer geek could lay out in minutes.

Keep in mind that you are borrowing today's money to be paid by tomorrow's earnings. The lender has to be convinced of the potential profitability of your business plans. This is in addition to having faith in your 5 *Cs* (see chapter 4).

Financial Statements

The financial statements are the documents produced to summarize the accounting activities of a cycle following a reporting format in compliance with the GAAP. A chartered accountant usually does the preparation as discussed in chapter 2. He or she can help you to understand the importance of the different entries. The most important is that the statements are accurate and balanced.

As the business owner, you must have a basic understanding of the reports because you have to be able to read and interpret the entries, especially during business planning for the future. The financial statements are the necessary evils that must be prepared at any cost because the revenue department of the government requires it. This is the number one reason other than evaluating the performance of your business.

There are reasons for learning and understanding the contents of financial statements, but they are mainly for your own consumption. The preparation of it is for the use of others such as investors, prospective buyers, and several government agencies like labor and consumers' affairs.

Here is an experience of a businessperson with an accountant.

The son of an immigrant businessperson finally got his license as an accountant. After analyzing the business practices of his father, the son commented, "The way you are keeping records—how would you know if you are making a profit?"

The father replied, "When I arrived in this country, I had nothing. Now I have a paid-up house and car plus a few thousand of savings; add them to all the things you see around you, subtract the value of my suitcase on arrival, which is negligible, and that, my son, is what you call profit!"

If only business life could be that simple!

The following pages are examples of balance sheets, income statements, and cash flows from operating expenses. As stated in the previous chapters, business is the movement of cash. This is a mandatory requirement in the submissions to the tax revenue department.

This should confirm in no uncertain terms the significance and importance of cash flow in relation to a successful business.

While the government revenue agency is concerned with the sources and uses of cash, your main interest is the presence and strength of cash flow like the human heartbeat. Is it regular with a steady beat or palpitating erratically, or worst, is it faint and inaudible?

The cash flow report could reveal the business pulse beat.

BALANCE SHEET
March 31, 2008
FREDERIC EMPLOYMENT AGENCY INC.
Incorporated under the laws of Ontario

	2007	2006
ASSETS		
Current		
Cash & Bank	$ 175,180	84,629
Accounts Receivable	111,208	166,796
Income Tax Receivable	-	21,896
Prepaid Expenses	9,975	11,821
Loan Receivable	717,453	572,406
	1,013,816	857,548
Capital (see note)	43,688	56,247
Other (see note)	425	425
	$ 1,057,929	914,220
LIABILITIES		
Current		
Accounts Payable	52,830	76,763
Income Tax Payable	29,944	-
Loan Payable	12,361	992
	94,865	77,755
SHAREHOLDERS' EQUITY		
Capital Stock	100	100
Retained Earnings	963,144	836,365
	$ 1,057,929	914,220

STATEMENT OF RETAINED EARNINGS
For the year ended March 31, 2007

FREDERIC EMPLOYMENT AGENCY INC.
Incorporated under the laws of Ontario

	2007	2006
Balance, Beginning of the Year	$ 836,365	810,728
Net Income for the Year	126,779	25,637
Balance, End of the Year	$ 963,144	836,365

STATEMENT OF INCOME
For the year ended March 31, 2007
FREDERIC EMPLOYMENT AGENCY INC.
Incorporated under the laws of Ontario

	2007	2006
Service Revenue	$ 2,178,656	$ 2,799,632
Direct Wages and Benefits	1,710,632	2,401,526
Gross Margin	468,024	398,106
Other Income	12,913	23,950
	480,937	422,056
Operating Expenses		
Management Remuneration	200,000	243,000
Advertising and Promotion	28,891	33,384
Office and General	18,981	22,484
Travel	16,095	16,682
Insurance	15,689	20,642
Amortization	14,693	20,335
Telephone/Postages	9,058	8,301
Accounting and Legal	7,651	7,025
Rent	6,000	6,000
Automobile Expenses	4,974	5,477
Interest and Bank Charges	2,530	5,013
	324,644	388,343
Net Income before Taxes	156,273	33,713
Income Tax Expense	(29,494)	(8,076)
NET INCOME	$ 126,779	$ 25,637

STATEMENT OF CASH FLOWS
For the year ended March 31, 2007
FREDERIC EMPLOYMENT AGENCY INC.
Incorporated under the laws of Ontario

	2007	2006
Cash Flows from Operating Activities	$ 126,779	25,637
Net Income for the Year		
Charges Not Affecting Cash Outlay	14,393	20,335
Amortization		
	141,472	45,972
Net Change in Non-Cash Working Capital		
Balances Related to Operations		
Accounts Receivable	55,588	(9,853)
Income Taxes Receivable	21, 896	21,896)
Prepaid Expenses and Deposits	1,846	667
Loan Receivable	(145,047)	(536,931)
Accounts Payable & Accrued Liabilities	(23,933)	69,148
Income Taxes Payable	29,494	(30,929)
Loan Payable	11,369	80
	92,685	(843,742)
Cash Flow from Investing Activities		
Acquisition of Capital Assets	(2,134)	-
Net Increase in Cash	90,551	(484742)
Cash, Beginning of the Year	84,629	568,371
Cash, End of the Year	$ 175, 180	84,629

Money Advice

The preceding tables are formats you could use in the service industry. Remember the accounting format you have to use depends on the industry you like to engage in. The GAAP applicable differs from one industry to the next simply because of the different entries needed.

Keep in mind that success is not dependent on how smart your presentations are but how you use the facilities and faculties you have effectively.

CHAPTER 8

Conclusion

The paramount responsibility of an individual is to have enough financial resources to pay for the cost of one's daily needs. This is accomplished by knowing the process of wealth accumulation, a difficult undertaking especially for the inexperienced. When you listen to the news on television or read the newspapers, you will find a long list of people and companies having financial difficulties, declaring bankruptcy, or closing shops.

If the absence of or just insufficient money is the problem, why then can't we simply raise more? It is a simple solution to a complex problem because the process of earning funds is as intricate and arduous as digging for the mother lode in a rocky mountain. To complicate matters, how do we know which of the whole host of ways of gaining money is appropriate for us?

The process of wealth accumulation is like picking the right arrangements from the 43,252,003,274,489,856,000 (about 43 quintillion) possible combinations of the 3x3x3 Rubik's Cube dilemma. A few wizards have mastered the algorithm of the puzzle, proving that there is a way. We just have to be curious and eager to learn.

While curiosity may kill the cat, it is the bare necessity for learning the intricacies of wealth accumulation. You have to be inquisitive. Ask anybody willing to help and give the answer most especially from the horse's mouth—money itself.

The first six chapters have been an eye-opener that if money could talk, the ideas raised should be sufficient to open the starting gate and get familiar with the rules of wealth accumulation.

The most important decree is the monetary golden tenet, which is, "he who has the gold makes the rules." Consider the following.

If you happen to be an insomniac watching television from midnight to the wee hours of the morning, chances are in flipping the channels you will come across some infomercials about how to become filthy rich, sleazy videos about females gone wild, or where to find the perfect person for your life.

These programs are designed to be an answer to your dreams; that is why they are aired at a time when you are either half or fast asleep. The message the producers want you to have resonates more easily in your subconscious mind when you are incapable of objecting to their sales pitch. They flavor their presentations with subliminal messages filled with nice-looking ladies attracted to your financial plans and success.

One particular program showed a Vietnamese young lad who seemed to have mastered the eloquence to relate his financial acumen in the good old USA. To emphasize the point, he was shown driving a Rolls-Royce with the top down and several shapely, scantily clad young girls enjoying the ride.

"I did it all by smartly investing in real estate," he proudly stated. "I did it without using money of my own because I had no job. I am living the American dream." If your salivary glands are not excited and overflowing with envy by such claims, you must have been desensitized by a tranquilizer or sleeping pills.

He surely did not look as if he had just gotten off from a rusty boat from Ho Chi Minh City, for he had the eloquence of Demosthenes and a polished thespian to express himself par excellence. He had to consciously guard his expressions and to inject his unmistakable Vietnamese diction lest he could be regarded as fake as snow in New York in mid-July. It looks like he didn't just pick up his command of the English language talking to GIs at the Hanoi Hilton.

If your interest was not sufficiently aroused at this time, there were testimonials from practitioners of the art of the real estate deal. There was a happy couple enjoying their swimming pool at the back of their semipalatial home in an unmistakably affluent neighborhood. There was a parade of people claiming to have metamorphosed from a meager existence to the land of abundance. All you have to do is follow the financial formula recommended by the gentleman from Vietnam.

What is the magical formula? Buy real estate with very low or nothing down, apply your carpentry and artistic skill, and sell the property at a hefty price, leaving you with a sizable profit. You can do this as often as your heart desires, in between pleasure trips and conventions with your fellow overachievers.

Is there a caveat to this?

First, you have to realize that the operators make money by charging for training courses. The program operators conduct and publish the materials. They claim to know how to get hold of the listings of depressed properties, foreclosures, powers of sale, distressed owners, and real estate repossessed by municipalities for nonpayment of taxes, all at a hefty price.

Assuming for the sake of argument that you are indeed successful in purchasing these properties, can you really turn around immediately and sell them for a fast buck? Are your eyes as sharp as an eagle's while others are blind as a bat?

The question is this: Who are you going to sell their property to? Is it to a sharp-eyed investor or to an investor whose vision relies on echoes in the dark? P. T. Barnum said that there is one born every minute of the day. It should not be difficult.

Second, what happens if you are stuck with properties? Can you maintain them financially and physically? Are you cut out to be a landlord? Do you enjoy fixing what others broke or cleaning up their messes?

Ah! That is what property managers are for! There are brokers willing and ready to help with an open palm. Really! Isn't a broker the one who will make you go broke?

God does not make land anymore! That is a powerful motivational phrase. It's true, but many a fortune has been buried in them. Speculations are not for amateurs, a sage investor once said.

All of these programs are in the business of conducting seminars. Robert Kiyosaki has joined the line of scrimmage, and Donald has upped the ante by charging admission upfront. He does not tease your palate with a free seminar. Television advertising and billboards warn the whole city of his coming like a messiah. The spirit of Paul Revere is on a limousine screaming, "The Donald is coming." Donald said in an interview that "people like me because I am successful in everything I do!" We like Donald for his flamboyance.

If Money Could Talk

We would like some of his financial talisman to stroke our flagging fortune to spring into action. Now he is the president of the United States.

We all wish to have Donald's personality and good looks. Well, maybe not his hair. But who could argue about Melania or the Miss Universe contestants.

To have a whole floor of a condominium in Manhattan is a magnet to nice ladies, even to the pure in heart. Who would not like to have that? But what can we do when the words "you're fired" are threatening to alter our financial security?

For sure President Trump gave something back for all the wealth he has. Some may be inherited, but we are sure that his ingenuity, flamboyance, perseverance, and personality played an important role; that is why he is wallowing in luxury. He also worked hard to win the presidency.

The message of this book is really simple. Money can only be earned by giving back the equivalent value of goods or services! This is what this book is all about. One could argue that a book like this is making a long story short. Who would not agree with that?

This book is not intended to be the only book you will ever need. Life is a continuous process of learning. However, one must start with the right basic knowledge; otherwise, life can become a litany of errors.

The fastest runner is not necessarily the Olympic champion for the hundred-meter dash. He or she is the one who also mastered the starting gate. Ask Usain Bolt of Jamaica, the sprinter, and he will confirm that.

With today's technology, he may also have the best running shoes and be the owner of finely engineered footwear, contrary to the belief of Bon Jovi.

The training for any competition is to master the fundamental principles first. Then the craft has to be honed to perfection by practicing frequently. Consistent practice makes perfect is advice adhered to strictly by champions.

If you want to be a professional singer, the do re mi of singing has to be adopted by your vocal cords; otherwise, the voice box will not produce the right melodic frequencies and tones. Besides, there has to be a conscious effort to safeguard the larynx from injuries. Remember—your vocal cords will be your cash register, and they require your constant vigil; otherwise, the thief of the night will steal your prized possession.

Like many of the skills we want to adopt and master, there are always discomforts and difficulties, especially at the beginning. This is referred to as the learning curve. The muscles needed for the desired expertise must be flexible enough to stretch and bend for a smooth performance.

Likewise, the art of earning money is to fully comprehend the basic theorem of money earning. If we do not learn the lessons well, then a chronic shortage of money is like a monkey on our backs.

Time

It is humorous when you hear that indolent people have no time to allocate for productive activities like learning a profitable skill, yet they are periodically inactive or engaged in wasteful pursuits. Keep in mind that the only thing you cannot recycle is wasted time.

Visit a third world country, and you will see many of the citizens seated comfortably on the ground with both arms embracing their folded knees staring and mentally counting the passersby. They are nonchalant, seemingly content, waiting for a shoe full of grace to drop.

That time is something we desperately want to have in order to waste is a common theme of human activities.

There are many maxims about time! Let us examine a few.

1. "Time and tide wait for no man": This should be the guiding principle to the procrastinators and the group who wait for things to happen.
2. "Time is a great healer": This is the panacea for the aches and pains we get when we experience setbacks due to failure. This motto might cause nightmares for our medical practitioners. Is this why time is not listed in the compendium of pharmaceuticals or drug references?
3. "Time will tell": What will time inform us of? In this journey we call life, the busloads of accomplishments have left without us.

It is time to make sure that our gunpowder is dry. It is time to rub our hands to gesture our readiness to forge ahead and declare to the world that we have run out of excuses! "The time has come!"

Success

"Every man is his own worst enemy" is a proverb that was as true before as it is now. Can you imagine that our fiercest nemesis is encased in our own selves? You cannot turn or run away from yourself. How could you?

The adversary is closer to you than your shadow. It follows you like the shirt on your back. Instead of imitating and seeing the same things, worst of all, it controls you like Mesmer with his subjects.

While poverty is not against the law, if you haven't ventured anything, you will gain nothing; that proverbial wisdom should motivate you in times of desperation. If you did not sow any seed, what will germinate?

The habit of success, especially in wealth accumulation, is a lifelong endeavor. It should be an ingrained attitude, entrenched in your beliefs and evident in your actions.

There are people whose households are disorganized where confusion is a mild description. Rooms, especially of teenagers, have items scattered all over the floor, rubbish for decorations, and refuse for accents! The habit of confusion is contraindicated to the formula of success in amassing considerable assets. Well-laid-out plans sometimes fail, let alone disorganized ones.

The habit of success should be practiced in everything we do. It should be second nature. It should be as easy and simple as ABC.

The Alphabets of Success

Attitude

Attitude is the dean of all qualifications of people most likely to succeed with whatever they wish in life. It is an accurate barometer of the ability to work with others. Your acceptability as a reliable businessperson or employee depends on it.

A healthy attitude is the most important qualification employers look for in their prospective employees.

Attitude is the most important requirement, more than work experiences, educational attainments, and capabilities.

The following chart summarizes the points.

Capabilities	Attitudes	Status
Best	Best	Hired
Best	Bad	Reject
Average	Best	Has Possibilities
Limited	Best	Maybe
Average/Limited	Bad	Reject

The above chart clearly indicates that a bad attitude will always lead to a polite "thank you" or "do not call us; we'll call you." Job applicants with average or limited capabilities can be considered for jobs of lesser responsibilities. There are job positions available for people with pleasant attitudes, even if their capabilities are below average.

They have fewer chances of being escorted to the exit door. Perhaps this is because people with average or limited capabilities could be helped and educated, but people with bad attitudes are construed as liabilities and could only be reformed in a correctional facility.

Many motivational gurus like Napoleon Hill, Norman Vincent Peale, and Dale Carnegie are the granddaddies of influencing our attitudes. They have written numerous books on the subject, specifically on a positive mentality.

You can fill a gymnasium of modern-day motivation maharishis like Anthony Robbins running to the stage like a baseball pitcher who could not wait to strike out a diamond ace. They flash warm smiles like Joel Scott Osteen, exposing dental work that is the delight of toothpaste manufacturers. They make energized voices at decibel levels that incite the crowds to religious fervor like Rev. Robert Schuler of the Crystal Cathedral in Garden Grove, California.

Their aim is to inspire the audience to exhibit positive mental attitudes, albeit ephemerally. It is their hope that you go home with a permanent motivation hangover that stays with you even at your sober moments.

In between the lectures of these sage motivation experts, some booster dose of wisdom will rejuvenate your flagging enthusiasm. Reading books like this one hopefully can help to stimulate you into action.

Attitude can be influenced, but the desire must be internally produced! You have to believe.

Belief

A standup comic asked during his monologue, "Why are those religious fanatics close to God? It is because every time they knock on your door early on a Sunday morning, they are close to death."

Why would people risk humiliation and ridicule to spread what they believe in? Even when they make a mistake of incorrectly predicting the end of the world, they are pounding the pavement the following day to warn us of the next doomsday. For the nonbelievers of faith and members of nonprophet organizations, it is difficult to comprehend the rationale of such behaviors.

The valedictorians of all militant believers are the kamikazes and suicide bombers. They are willing to make the ultimate sacrifice, which literally puts an end to their lives. The Japanese did the dastardly act for the love of their emperor. The suicide bombers are doing it for the promise of the company of seventy-two vestals upon arrival at the promised land. The same commitment should be adopted in our quest for wealth.

Belief in the unknown is a difficult undertaking, after all, for to see is to believe. It is the confidence we have in the undertaking, especially if it is given to us by a system we favor or somebody we respect.

Successful teachers and religious leaders work hard on perfecting this principle of making themselves believable. Confidence artists (con artists) work even harder at cultivating this credible trust to perfect their craft.

Once belief in something is established in our conscious and subconscious minds, raging infernos cannot dissuade us from accomplishing whatever we set ourselves up to do.

Just like the proverbial postmen who will brave the fiercest storm, sleet, or snow, vicious dogs and jealous husbands cannot prevent them from doing their appointed rounds of pushing the envelopes into your mailboxes.

That is because these letter carriers believe in the importance of their jobs, and, most especially, they are committed to their work. Really! Just ask any one of them.

Commitment

"The last time I made a commitment, I had to swear for it in front of a minister by pledging, 'I do'"—a funny comment by a comic who we are sure was left standing for the last time. His better half got the other half of him for sure.

No wonder only a few people will commit to anything. It is scary! It has the ring of finality to it. If you are agreeing with a commitment that makes the other party complete, and you are finished, only a few will survive to tell the tale.

The seal of commitment is affixed only when we are assured albeit with room for doubt that beyond the clouds are silver linings.

The ability to make decisions (see the sales and marketing chapter) eases the trauma of commitment! We cannot make decisions if we are not well versed in the terms of the agreement!

Dedication, Desire, and Decision

In the drag racing of wealth accumulation, dedicated desire is the high octane petroleum that kick-starts our revving egos. Without a burning rubber of desire, we will not go to the starting mark, let alone accelerate to the finish line.

Chapter 2 discussed decision-making abilities as a requirement to business success; a strong desire will make us decide to commit to the program of wealth accumulation. They all go hand in hand.

People who make decisions that oscillate like a pendulum change their decisions every minute, which makes your head spin. It shows that in making the decision, there was no dedication, desire, and energy.

Energy

You eat to have energy and to fuel the body with energy, but if you do not have the money to buy the food, then how can you gas up your empty tank? Another case of contradiction is in the making.

Successful people seem to have inexhaustible reserves of energy. They are like the Energizer bunny who never stops doing or accomplishing something. Can this feeling be contagious? It is, if you have faith.

Faith

Faith is the belief in something that has no scientific proof. Sometimes they are interchangeable, but for our purposes, we shall define belief as something we trust as truth, while faith is belief in ourselves. If we do not have faith in our abilities, who will?

An excellent philosophy is to let others fail us, but we should never fail ourselves. Other people will always discredit our capabilities; critics are a dime a dozen. Leave them alone, and do not join the fray.

We should be critical of our accomplishments, but it is not wise to be doubtful of our own abilities. The former makes us wiser and better while the latter makes us quitters.

Goal Setting

The ultimate goal of baseball is to hit a ball the size of an average fist being hurled to you at an average speed of over eighty miles per hour. In basketball, the goal is to shoot a ball through a rim eighteen inches in diameter. In both cases, the objectives are to hit or shoot the ball with or to a target of limited dimension. The hitting or shooting act should be precise; otherwise, the result will be a miss.

Coaches devise techniques that increase the players' odds of hitting or shooting the ball. The science of successful playing is not haphazard preparation but a carefully drawn plan.

All commercial airplanes are equipped with an automatic direction finder (ADF) that displays a dial showing a needle pointing at the destination airport. The objective is just a small dot on the map, and a small angle of deviation will mislead the plane. Goals are like that. Unless precisely laid out, they will end up at a different destination.

Goal-Setting Cycle

What is wrong with goal statements like "I want to be rich," "I want to be successful," and "I want to be the best"? These are ambiguous general declarations devoid of specifics that the human mind cannot implement however well intentioned the planner may be.

Simply saying you want to be rich is so nebulous that the subconscious mind cannot act upon it. It is not sufficient because the exact amount of wealth wanted is not defined. The time frame of accomplishment is not mentioned. More importantly, what you are willing to give back is not stated.

For the omissions stated above, the mind can settle with any amount, small or large. The destination was not mentioned, so how will it know when you get there? For your purposes, you may already be there. You have to be precise in what you want.

After all, you have to be clear when you want the desired amount in your possession. Acting without a deadline makes the mind procrastinate, since there is no time frame stated in the plan.

The most important omission is the cost you are willing to pay for the goal.

Here is a sample of a workable goal.

> At my fortieth birthday, I want to have saved up in my bank the amount of $1,000,000, have a monthly income of $25,000 (interest/investment and salary), have a house worth $500,000 in today's dollars, and have a car valued at $50,000.
>
> For this goal, I am willing to do the following: (make a list of all the things you plan to do and accomplish).

You can check your daily progress and make necessary adjustments. Remember your goal is a legal contract with yourself, minus the legal parlance and fine print. Make it binding and ironclad.

Your Own Inspiration Words

Stop at goal setting, for one of the exercises is to fill the rest of the alphabet with your favorite words of wisdom that have been your inspirations and guides. Remember that words will not work unless you do. They open your mind to infinite possibilities, but like a parachute, it is useless when closed.

Keep dreaming, but make sure you do not oversleep; you may wake up with regrets and realize that life is too short to recover and has flown away like a balloon in the sky.

Finally, Back to Basics

Albert Einstein advised us that if we want to get a different result of what we are doing, change the process used. This sensible remark should have a stronger blast than the atomic bomb that resulted from his theory of relativity. These words of wisdom have more desirable effects on our lives than the explosions in Nagasaki and Hiroshima. Einstein's theory of insanity benefits humankind more than his theory of relativity.

The reason for this lunacy is the refusal to learn and to get back to the basics and fundamentals of wealth accumulation. Financial difficulties are pervasive from the rural areas of the third world to the urban centers of the industrialized countries, yet there is no lobby group dedicated to changing the attitudes of the needy. Instead, the blame is placed squarely on the shoulders of the affluent with the firm belief that the Robin Hood formula of assets redistribution is a foolproof solution. Some countries have experimented with land reforms without making a dent on the census of the financially dislocated populace.

Technology, especially in the fields of communication and electronics in the last fifty years, is far more advanced than it was in the previous centuries combined, yet the economic standard of people has been getting worse. Everyone believes that the rich are getting richer and the poor are getting poorer. Is this the gospel truth or just a justification for reform?

The less fortunate members of society are no longer isolated from the dissemination of information. Pictures in living color on plasma televisions broadcast the vision of affluence enjoyed by the privileged few. The ubiquitous cell phone equipped with cameras and text messages updates the less fortunate with the latest gadgets. Wireless equipment is now a necessity instead of a luxury.

Even remote areas of the world are now connected electronically via the internet, which could be advantageous or a source of frustration. This is precisely why the former communist countries of Europe could no longer contain their citizens from revolting. The beneficial effects of wealth cannot be camouflaged from view. Every citizen wants a piece of the proverbial pie. However, one must be aware of the cost.

Therefore, if money could talk, it would remind us of the following.

The basis of wealth accumulation is to understand that money is a mere representation of goods or services, as explained in the beginning of this book. It is worth repeating that if you think of money, you are looking not at a rectangular piece of currency but at the goods or services given or produced in return.

The process of acquiring the knowledge of wealth accumulation is learned in small steps, not in giant leaps. There are many books written to help and guide you to the financial bonanza. With the myriad published materials, choosing the one appropriate for you is an art by itself. You could end up educated or disappointed, depending on your understanding and ability to implement the principles you just learned.

A case in point: unless you have billions of dollars to invest, you could not emulate Warren Buffett's investment style and strategy. Buffett will not invest in a company without gaining control and direct participation in the management of the target company. This means that Warren and his entourage must have a firm grip on the bird in hand, not merely a bird's-eye view. The board of directors will only invite you to the annual shareholders' meeting if you own some shares but will politely dismiss your unwanted questions. The difference is that Buffett gives ulcers to the board, while the company directors have the propensity to give you one.

Likewise, should you want your son or daughter to begin to learn tennis, it is irrational to hire Roger Federer to be the instructor, even if Roger agrees and you can afford the costs of championship lessons.

This is like hiring a person with a doctoral degree to teach kindergarten lessons to your child.

Severin Luthi, Federer's head coach, may be a better instructor, especially when the student has mastered the fundamentals and acquired the tennis discipline and is ready to join the Wimbledon parade. The general rule is to bite the size you could swallow; otherwise, you could choke. Sage advice is that a journey of a thousand miles starts with the first step.

When is the best time to engage yourself in business? Anytime that you are infected with the entrepreneurial bug is the best time. If you keep your managerial acumen in constant loop, one of these days it will receive an interrupt that will branch into a lucrative program. When will it happen? Who knows? It can be any day, any time, but you will know as soon as it shows, like the lyrics of a song from *Westside Story*.

Finally, let me reiterate that this is the first step to awaken your dormant mind to succeed and start the wonderful world of money accumulation. A success formula does not necessarily work all the time, because you may need constant practice to perfect the process. Remember there is nothing better than an idea whose time has come!

For *pecuniae cause*, you will find out that money is not taciturn or expressionless.

Money, if it could communicate, actually speaks volumes.

APPENDIX

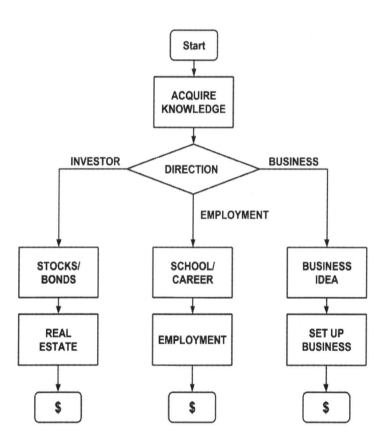

Figure 11

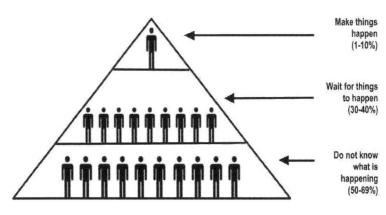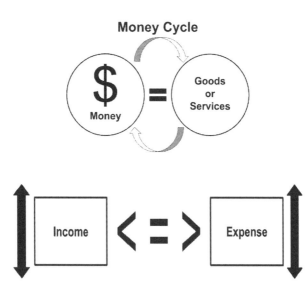

Pacific Book Review
helping authors succeed!

www.pacificbookreview.com

Title: If Money Could Talk **Author:** M.L. Marcos
Publisher: iUniverse **ISBN:** 978-1-5320-6717-4
Pages: 221
Genre: Economics
Reviewed by: Carl Conrad

Pacific Book Review

In a book that will entertain you with anecdotes and brief profiles of famous people at the same time as it acquaints you with the various functions, uses, and purposes of money, M.L. Marcos' book, *If Money Could Talk,* will also offer you direct knowledge of how to startup, finance, operate, and maintain a business from his more than thirty years of experience from having done so. With lessons, examples, slogans, and lots of encouragement, the author methodically and comprehensively takes the reader on a journey to learn the valuable lessons of what money could tell us, if money could talk.

His primary purpose, and repeatedly useful notion to drive home, was the point that the value of money is equal to the value of the goods and services it represents. This means that the balance between how much money is created and how many goods and services are available can be influenced by either creating more money – which, without a corresponding increase in goods and services, devalues the amount of money available, often called "inflation" – or by creating more goods and services – which, without a corresponding increase in money, increases the value of money which is often called "deflation". So it is this aggregate balance between the amount of money created and the amount of goods and services available that determines how many goods and services can be purchased with each unit of money.

Mr. Marcos goes on to describe the ways in which money is paid to us – through work, ownership, and investments – as well as the many types of businesses that can be created with it – proprietorships, partnerships, and corporations – then takes the reader on a long tour through the mechanics of business development in which he describes how a business evolves and matures, of course first starting with the creation of a business plan because, as he says: "If you start not knowing what to do, you could end up not knowing what you have done."

In an exhortation that "Chutzpah is the only qualification you will ever need," Mr. Marcos identifies subcategories such as; leadership, the ability to communicate, age and health factors, as well as characteristics like rhythm, and flamboyance that can propel a person into success as a business owner. He also deals with how to start a business, how to manage a business, and how to maintain a business in which he offers many concrete ideas about factors to be considered when deciding what business to start and what markets to operate in.

It is a fun book to read as it also shows off the tremendous number and variety of people in all walks of life whom Mr. Marcos uses as examples to illustrate his points from Bill Gates of Microsoft fame to some as obscure as Norma Desmond of *Sunset Boulevard* who can tell so much "with just one look" that he often dazzles you with the breadth of his knowledge and his practical advice.

If you are looking for a primer on all things business and money, *If Money Could Talk* is a book that will tell you as much as you want to hear.

The US Review of Books

If Money Could Talk
by M. L. Marcos
iUniverse

book review by Michelle Jacobs

"The process of acquiring the knowledge of wealth accumulation is learned in small steps, not in giant leaps."

This guide to financial freedom takes the mystery out of building wealth with its no-nonsense approach and practical insights. Marcos breaks down lessons on success and hones in on business development and entrepreneurship as a means to maximum wealth acquisition. The author first builds a foundation for understanding income sources and influences then launches into the various logistics of business development and management.

At the heart of this book is the message that people must be actively engaged in reaching "economic nirvana" by exploring and engaging with financial opportunities. Marcos believes that everyone has access to wealth if they are willing to participate in the pursuit. He hopes to level the playing field of wealth accumulation with this business guide.

Readable and engaging, this book covers a wide range of topics to motivate readers to take control of their financial futures through business endeavors. Marcos effectively and generously incorporates analogies, examples, and anecdotes to strengthen his message and keep it accessible to all readers interested in improving their financial lives. While business majors and budding entrepreneurs will find much clear-sighted guidance in this book, lay people looking to build fiscal confidence will also find what they need from Marcos. Combining practical topical advice with motivational verve, he covers the basics and beyond.

The chapters that provide counsel on financing a business and that offer helpful financial checklists solidify that the author wants to mentor those interested in actively pursuing personal wealth through their professional choices. In this role as a mentor and guide, Marcos becomes a mouthpiece for money, revealing what money would say *If Money Could Talk.*

ABOUT THE AUTHOR

Fred L. Marcos is a businessperson from 1981 to the present who has been involved in the setup, formation, and management of small businesses.

The main reason for this book is to leave a legacy to a sixteen-year-old son and to share the business experiences with others who can benefit from the author's observations and acquired knowledge.

Manufactured by Amazon.ca
Bolton, ON